To Barbara

"How we make sense of the major successes and losses in our lives determines what we think is important now."
– p. 9

with warm wishes

July 2/04

John Kuypers speaks from experience. In 1992, this driven, successful corporate executive collapsed on the family room floor at the age of thirty-four. It was the wake-up call that led him on a seven-year journey that would transform his life from an obsessive frenzy to one with a deep confidence and a clear sense of purpose. He walked away from a $250,000 income and a superficially happy marriage in order to discover for himself why he felt dissatisfied with his life. John Kuypers has become a success by a different means — by learning how to live in the present, free from second-guessing past decisions and from fretting over goals yet to be achieved. Today, he writes, teaches, and speaks to people from all walks of life about the rewards of a sharper mind, a healthier body and a sense of life that come with living more fully in

Please ... *re saying*
about ... *scovering*

What's Important Now

What's Important Now

Shedding the Past So You Can Live in the Present

John Kuypers

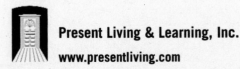

Present Living & Learning, Inc.
www.presentliving.com

Published by Present Living & Learning, Inc.

Burlington, ON Canada L7R 3X4
www.presentliving.com

National Library of Canada Cataloguing in Publication Data

Kuypers, John, 1957–

　　　What's important now: shedding the past so you can
　　　live in the present

Includes bibliographical references.

ISBN 0-9689684-0-6

1. Self-Help　2. Change　3. Self-actualization (Psychology)

I. Title

BF637.S4K89 2002　　　158.1　　　C2001-903541-1

The author wishes to express his appreciation to the following for the use of brief quotations from their material:

Getting the Love You Want, by Harville Hendrix, ©1988 by Harville Hendrix. Reprinted by permission of Henry Holt & Co., LLC.

Man's Search For Meaning, by Viktor E. Frankl, Copyright ©1959, 1962, 1984, 1992 by Viktor E. Frankl. Reprinted by permission of Beacon Press, Boston

Illuminata, by Marianne Williamson ©1994, Random House Publishers

The Holy Bible, New International Version. Copyright © 1973, 1978, 1984 by International Bible Society. Used by permission of International Bible Society. All rights reserved.

Cover/text design by Heidy Lawrance Associates
Manufactured in Canada

"Perhaps love is the process
of my leading you
gently back to yourself.
Not whom I want you to be,
but to who you are."

Antoine de Saint-Exupéry

Table of Contents

Introduction

If someone had asked me ten years ago if I was doing what was important, I would have answered with a resounding, "Yes!" After all, I was surrounded by the proof. I had a blossoming career, a good wife, a big house, successful friends, and all the money I needed. What more could a person want? Yet I did want more. I don't mean just the usual "faster car, bigger job, better sex life," kind of male dissatisfaction. Sure I would have taken more of those. But I felt an ache for something more. I wanted something that would give my life meaning. My success was not giving me the satisfaction and joy in life that I expected. I felt frightened by the idea that I might wake up one day at the age of seventy, with only a fat bank account and a weighty resumé to show for my entire life's efforts. For reasons I did not yet understand, that kind of a past would not have been good enough.

Several years later, a close friend of mine died unexpectedly. The depth of my grief in the face of his permanent departure staggered me. He was only forty-one! We had shared so many hopes and dreams beginning twenty years earlier as university roommates and later as business partners. His life stared back at me like a continuous-loop video. Did he have a full life? Was he happy? Did he achieve what he really wanted while he was alive? I had my doubts, but I'll never know. Death is so final. There is no tomorrow. There isn't even an extra five minutes.

These are the moments in life that hit us like a brick wall. We are shocked into the awareness that despite our brains and our toil, despite our giving and our loving, we may not have been doing what's truly important for us. We are faced with a certain harshness of knowing that we are not in control of our lives to the extent we would like to be. These events caused an alarm to go off in my head. Why am I never quite satisfied? What should I be doing in order to have no regrets when I am lying on my death bed?

If you are asking yourself these kinds of questions, this book is for you. In your dissatisfaction with your current situation lies the evidence that what you are doing, or how you are doing it, is not quite right for you. I discovered that my answers lay within me. All I had to do was dig them out, painfully and persistently. In the process, I learned how to live in the present, the most joyous and unexpected gift I could ever have imagined.

When you are present, your true self emerges, unfiltered and unguarded. This is an extraordinary way to discover who you are and what is right or wrong for you in any given moment. All of us have been tainted by our parents, friends, cultural norms, and past experiences to the extent that we end up living unconsciously and out of habit. We do what we've always done because it's familiar, even if it isn't necessarily what's right for us. When we truly know who we are, we can act with the confidence that we will do what's right for us, because that *is* what's important now.

This journey of self-discovery is like going through a series of dark and intimidating doorways set in an immense wall. When you approach one of these doorways, you will face the choice of crossing through or turning away. Each time you dare to go forward, you will discover a deeper sense of joy and acceptance of who you are as a person. As you grow to know and trust who you are, you will become capable of living more fully in the present. You open yourself to achieving extraordinary personal excellence because you are able to focus all of your mind and body, and all of your heart and soul on the present moment.

Discovering what's important now for you by living in the present is a gift to yourself and to everyone around you. There is no greater gift you can give others than to be fully present with them. They see it in your eyes. They hear it in your words. They feel it in their bones. You are with them, openly and non-judgmentally. You are giving them the most loving thing you can give another human being. You are also doing the most loving thing that you can do for yourself.

The following poem captures the attitude of someone who wants to live with the sure confidence that they are doing what's important now for them. This poem was inscribed on a sign on the wall of Mother Theresa's children's home in Calcutta, India. It exhorts each of us to be true to ourselves in every moment, despite the obstacles that will most certainly come our way on the journey of life. May it inspire you as it inspires me.

John Kuypers
October 2001

ANYWAY

People are often unreasonable, illogical
and self-centered. Love them anyway.

If you are kind, people will accuse you of selfish,
ulterior motives. Be kind anyway.

If you are successful, you will win some false
friends and some true enemies. Succeed anyway.

If you are honest and frank, people may cheat
you. Be honest and frank anyway.

What you spent years building may be
destroyed overnight. Build anyway.

If you find serenity and happiness, they may be
jealous. Be happy anyway.

The good you do today will often be forgotten
tomorrow. Do good anyway.

Give the world the best you have and it may
never be enough.

Give the world the best you've got anyway.

You see, in the final analysis, it is between
you and God.

It was never between you and them anyway.

Prologue: The Journey

FUEL FOR THE JOURNEY

If you want to discover the personal excellence that comes from shedding the past so you can live in the present, you have to know what that looks like and feels like for you. You will recognize it as those times when you felt that you were at your best, regardless of whether you were immersed in your favorite activity, or surviving a disaster. You must rekindle your memories of those times in order to provide fuel for your journey towards knowing and doing what's important now for you.

I want to share with you an experience that kept my desire to discover what was right for me alive over many years. I had a magical time when I was twenty-three years old. For nearly two years, I soared with a deep joy and confidence, accomplishing more than I ever dreamed possible for a Dutch immigrant farmer's son. My soaring began when I was fresh out of university with a business degree in hand. I was starting my dream career as a marketing whiz kid-in-training with a multinational consumer products company. Within less than a month of starting the job, I was on the company jet with the president of the U.S. division. Already, I was a big wheel! Six months later, I completed my sales training in Montreal. Not only did I become fluently bilingual, I over-achieved on all my sales targets. When I returned to the head office in Toronto, I had already developed a reputation as a "shooter". My confidence soared even more when I took an assertiveness training course—just to accompany my somewhat timid girlfriend. To my great surprise, I was the one who really benefited.

I especially noticed the effects at work. For a twenty-three year old guy, I sounded as if I actually knew how to run the multi-million dollar slice of business on which I was a mere product assistant. I was decisive and I had good ideas. I was also learning at a phenomenal pace. At the end of each work day, I felt that I had great clarity about what I had done well or not. I could see clearly the changes that I wanted to make in how I did my job. I applied those changes the very next day. My bosses were impressed. I was pretty impressed myself.

Even if I made a mistake or offered up a dumb idea, I felt unperturbed. My managers viewed me as a rising star. They seemed to see only my positive qualities. The more they believed in me, the more I believed in myself. I had a tremendous feeling of ownership concerning the product that I was working on. I lay awake at night, thinking about ways in which I could motivate Canadians to buy more of my company's brand of fabric softener. Many of my ideas were well received. I was rewarded with two promotions and numerous pay raises within my first two years.

Sometimes I wondered how I could have become such a successful, popular guy, when I had always thought of myself as a loser. I decided that if I had been able to get this far, I must be capable of being anyone I wanted to be. All I had to do was put my mind to it. Somehow my hard work and determination had made me a hotshot businessman. There was no other way in which I could explain my unexpected and extraordinary success.

My success did not stop at the office door, either. That same summer of 1981, I played softball for the company baseball team. I had never been a great hitter. In a good year, I would hit around .300. That summer I was on fire. I finished the year batting .490 against some excellent pitchers. I was the top offensive player on our team and one of the top hitters in the league. I seemed to perform especially well when we were under pressure, making clutch hits that won games for us.

Socially, I developed many new friendships. Whether it was business lunches, parties, or interdepartmental baseball games, I was a well-liked and popular guy. Women were attracted to me, although I didn't do any dating. I was still feeling too wounded from my recently failed relationship.

Sometimes I felt as if I were living in someone else's body. It was as if I had entered a whole new world, where I had checked out my old brain at the door, and put on a new one instead. My old brain said I was a loser. My new brain said I was a winner. I made a concerted effort not to think about my success. I was afraid that thinking about it would jinx it. I found myself accepting my performance as if it were the most natural thing in the world, even though a little voice inside me was having its doubts. Could this really be happening to *me*? Yet I felt a growing confidence that it would last. I just kept hitting like a machine—on the field, at work, and socially.

At the end of the season, we were in the final game of the playoffs. We were losing and we weren't getting any runs. I was late for the game and the coach was visibly annoyed with me. He decided to leave me on the bench. When the fifth inning began, I could hear some of my teammates muttering just loudly enough for him to hear, "C'mon coach, we've got our best hitter sitting on the bench. Watcha' doing, coach?"

Finally, the coach relented. I got up to bat. Same confidence. Same "I've got all the time in the world to hit this baby" kind of feeling. On the third pitch, I cracked the ball to a hole in center field and raced down the path to first base. Boy, did I feel some satisfaction in that moment. Not about rubbing it in my coach's face. But rather that I had come through in the crunch. I really loved myself in that moment. No ego stuff. Just self-trust. I could count on me.

The next season began with high hopes and high expectations. I felt quite nervous. There was a voice inside my head asking the same question over and over: "Can I do it again?" The thought of not being able to repeat my star performance scared me. Everyone on the team and even everyone in the company was now aware that I was a "great" hitter. I desperately wanted to live up to their expectations. As the season unfolded, my fears came true. I lost my touch. I struck out a lot. I hit directly into the opposing team's fielders. I felt my spirits sink deeper and deeper. A little voice inside my head said it all. "See, you really are a loser."

Meanwhile, back at the office, I grew dissatisfied with my job. Despite my rapid ascent up the corporate ladder, I decided that the company was not growing fast enough to meet my ever-expanding expectations. At twenty-four, I was pretty sure I knew how to run the company. Despite that, top management still kept doing things the same old way. I convinced myself that I had to find a new job with a more aggressive company.

I left that job in my third year. On my first day at the new job, my heart sank. I immediately knew that I had not done what was right for me. Suddenly, I saw all the warts of the new company. It lacked the positive spirit and supportive environment of my old company. Only then did I fully appreciate the good things about my first job. I spent seven miserable months with that second company before leaving to begin an entirely different career adventure. After eight months, that move did not work out, either. To my delight, one of the managers at my first company offered to hire me back. I decided to accept, grateful for a second chance. But I just didn't feel the same. After two "failed" career moves, my confidence was deeply shaken. I felt embarrassed that I had gone crawling back to my first job. After just four months, I made my fourth career move in a year and a half, determined to make it a success. I stayed with that company for the next nine years.

How we make sense of the major successes and losses in our lives determines what we think is important now for us. When we make the "right" moves, we are brimming with confidence, certain of who we are, what we want and how we are doing it. When we make "mistakes", experience "failure" and "tragedy", we open ourselves to self-doubt. When good things happen, we soar. When bad things happen, we crash. Our sense of peace, our sense of happiness, and our sense of self-worth are inextricably interwoven with what's happening around us. We know something's wrong yet we are unclear about what it is because we are depending on events outside of ourselves to give us our self-confidence.

I want to briefly review my magical year with you, so that you might appreciate the major themes of this book on discovering what's important for you, in the present moment. What happened that helped me feel confident, outgoing, and decisive? What happened that spun me into a cautious, conservative state of mind? If these themes stir you, then you will benefit greatly from learning how to live more fully in the present.

First of all, I felt that I had the permission, support, and encouragement of my managers and my colleagues to be the best I could be, mistakes and all. Feeling accepted is the core foundation to finding the courage to be who we really are, in the moment. However, I depended on other people for that. *We need to learn how to feel accepted within ourselves, even when other people no longer give us the support they once did.*

Taking the assertiveness course also helped me tremendously. I began to believe that I was entitled to have opinions, feelings, and desires, even if other people disagreed. I became willing to speak up, without fearing that someone might ridicule me or that I might lash out at them for disagreeing with me. *We must have the courage to say and do what's right for us despite experiences in the past when doing so felt dangerous.*

Ironically, my success became a barrier to living in the present. I became so convinced of my brilliance at work that I wanted to do more than I had the right or the responsibility to do. I did not accept that top management was doing the best they could. I wanted them to run the company the way *I* thought they should. When I left that first job, I was hoping deep down that top management would be sorry I had left and would make changes to the company. When we pressure others to do what *we* think they should be doing, we are naturally led to become anxious or obsessive about it. *We need to learn how to do what's important for us without an intention to pressure others to change what they think is right for them.*

Even my baseball success led me to stop living in the present. I became so anxious about failing that my mind was no longer clear and empty, focused solely on the coming pitch. Instead, I felt self-conscious about what my teammates would think if I failed to get a hit each time. The more I struck out, the more I felt a self-imposed pressure to do even better the next time. Becoming anxious reduces our effectiveness, thereby *increasing* the likelihood that we will fail. *We need to learn to detach ourselves from future outcomes* *based on past results so that we can totally focus on what we are doing **now**.*

If you want the joy and the deep self-confidence that come with living in the present, take a moment right now and search your memory for those moments when you really loved who you were. Whether it was a day ago or a lifetime ago, allow the details to come into focus on the screen of your mind. Remember how good you felt about yourself. In those moments lay hidden the many secrets of how you were everything you wanted to be. Now you must learn how to extract those secrets without trying to reproduce the situation itself. That time is now over, yet that person who soared to great heights is still alive and well within you.

THE REWARDS

When you are living in the present, you *know* what's important for you, and you act on that knowing. You are able to see the big picture and the smallest detail all at the same time. Your sense of timing and your instincts become sharp. Time itself slows down and you adapt fluidly to the reality of the present moment. You become an extraordinary and powerful human being. Great athletes show us just how true this is. Even if you are not an athlete yourself, you can learn something from them. After all, no person's body is independent of their mind, their heart, or their soul. When you are fully present, all four of these dimensions of your humanness are operating in harmony, letting you be as excellent as you can be.

Wayne Gretzky has been hailed as the greatest hockey player who ever lived. Hockey experts often describe him as having a sixth sense. They say he could see the whole ice surface at once, recognize the pattern of how the play was unfolding, and intuitively make the right decision about where to pass or shoot the puck. By his own admission, he did not possess superior skating or shooting skills. Wayne Gretzky is simply an incredibly present athlete.

In the summer of 2000, Tiger Woods won the PGA championship, the only one of the four major championships he had yet to win. When asked afterwards how he handled the pressure of making a crucial chip shot on the last hole that ultimately led to his victory, he said, "I just tried to stay in the moment and focus on the shot I had to make." Tiger Woods did not let his mind drift to the importance of making that shot, or to worrying about what people would think if he failed. His entire being was focused on what was important for him in that moment.

At the 1999 World Track and Field Championships, Canadian sprinter Bruny Surin lost the one-hundred-metre dash to American Maurice Greene. Greene set a new world record of 9.79 seconds. However, Surin was leading the race for the first forty metres. When Surin was asked afterwards what happened at that moment in the race, he said that he became aware that he was beating Greene and became elated at the possibility that he might actually win. At that moment, Greene raced past him to win gold and set a new world record. Surin had let his mind drift to the future, a future that was still five seconds away.

All great athletes describe their talents at the moment of truth with one common reality: Time slows down. Great home-run hitters say the baseball slows down for them, even though it is streaking in at over ninety miles per hour. They say that the ball looks like the size of a pumpkin. They feel they have lots of time to decide whether to swing or not. These athletes are incredibly present in those moments.

It is not that you and I don't know how to live in the present in our own less glamorous lives. We are often present when we are pursuing a favorite pastime or hobby. Gardening, cooking, watching a fire crackle, and mountain biking are just a few of the hundreds of ways in which we can get into times of flow that could be described as being fully present. The key question for you and me is whether we can create that same experience for ourselves when we feel under pressure. When the chips are down, our ability to be present measures whether we are able rise to our full potential. I learned a lesson on how we can do this from a professional basketball coach, long before I had heard of living in the present.

I was at a senior management meeting in Connecticut. Our president invited Pat Riley, then the coach of the NBA's New York Knicks, to speak to us. Pat Riley told us about the concept that he used with his players to get the best out of them:

W.I.N. What's Important Now.

I was struck by this simple idea. "What's Important Now" was Pat Riley's way of helping his players to be fully present while they were on the court. He talked about the distractions that his professional basketball players had to deal with—endorsements, business deals, contracts, money management, women, and so on. I could certainly imagine how easily any human being could get distracted by these seductive things, and how these distractions could reduce a person's effectiveness.

I was also impressed by one other aspect of What's Important Now. These were top players. Their skills were among the best in the world. They did not need a lot of skill-based teaching and instruction. What they needed was the right *attitude* to succeed. In Riley's experience, motivating his players to be present was the most powerful tool that he had to help them perform to the top of their game... to be the best they could be... superstars in their field. He knew they could achieve greatness if they devoted all of their mental, physical, emotional, and spiritual selves to that one thought: What's Important Now.

Is it any different for the rest of us? When we focus on What's Important Now, we become the best we can be during our own most challenging moments. Whether we are dealing with a rebellious child, persisting with an annoying repair job around the house, or leading an important business meeting, we are deciding that this activity is *the most important thing* we could be doing in our lives in this moment. We are not experiencing an urge to be somewhere else, to do something else, or to think about something else.

To achieve this wonderful state of mind, you must know who you are. You must trust yourself that you will do what is right for you, without having overly pre-planned your actions, and without the memory of past wounds holding you back. Mark Twain once said, "I have worried about a great many things in my life. And a few of them actually happened." To experience the joy, the self-confidence, and the excellence that comes with living in the present, you must find a way to let go of what you think *should* be happening, in order to immerse yourself in what *is* happening. The purpose of this book is to teach insights and techniques that will help you to uncover how your past is infiltrating and distorting your ability to *know* and *do* what's important now for you.

WHAT IS "THE PRESENT"?

The present is what is happening when you strip away all the resentments of your past and all the worries you have about your future. To live in the present is to live as if the past never existed and as if the future were irrelevant. Living in the present is a vision for life that is achievable in *any* moment, yet is unattainable in *every* moment. None of us is that perfect.

To live in that seemingly surreal state of mind requires one thing: a deep self-confidence that you are good enough. In order to live in the present, you must trust that you will be able to handle whatever comes your way, without undue thought or preparation. When we were toddlers around the age of two, we had that deep self-trust. We knew beyond a shadow of a doubt that we were good enough, because we had no concept that we could be anything else but good enough. We were at ease with who we were. We were open and curious about each new moment. We had no expectations about what was *supposed* to happen. We didn't judge events or people as good or bad, nor did we blame anyone. Instead, we adapted, showing our feelings in the moment and without reservation. Our joy was complete joy. Our anger and our tears were full and intense. We recovered from the setbacks of life in minutes. We were not self-conscious about what we were doing or about how we looked while doing it. Life was an adventure that we explored passionately and intensely.

As an adult seeking to know and do what's important now when facing uncertainty, you must rediscover this child-like state of mind. You will find it when you know in your heart that you are *already* prepared for this moment. Then you will be free to be true to who you really are at any-time, anywhere. Your joy will abound because you have no reason to fear what might happen if you make a mistake or if you don't do things the way someone else would want you to do them. You are good enough, even if others disagree.

When you do what's important now for you, you create a past that leaves you ready to handle the present. By default, the future is taking care of itself as you make decisions that are acceptable to you no matter what happens tomorrow. You no longer give yourself reasons to feel self-doubt, anxiety, or resentment. You are doing the best you can. You accept that what happens next is not in your control. You trust that you will handle whatever comes your way, no matter how fabulous or awful it may be.

When you are fully present, you are open and vulnerable. You say and do whatever comes to your mind without filtering it. You disclose your true feelings, right in the moment. You follow your inner spirit, trusting that you are doing what is right for you in that moment. If you don't get the result you wanted, you don't judge yourself or others as having failed. It's just what's happening in this moment. Your only question is, what's important for me in this new moment? In this way, your excellence is allowed to emerge from within you in ways that you may never have dreamed possible.

You might appreciate that this can also be a very dangerous way to live. You might say or do something that someone in your life is not going to like. You might offend someone important at work. You might do something impulsive, like having a sexual fling or quitting your job. You might spend yourself into a deep debt. You might even lose control of your emotions and do something vindictive or cowardly that you might later painfully regret. For these reasons, you need to feel very safe in order to dare to be present. When you expose who you really are, unfiltered and unguarded, you are very vulnerable. Is it a coincidence that we typically only show the "dark" side of our personalities to those whom we love the most? We don't yell at our boss or at our customers. We yell at our spouses, our children, and perhaps our employees. We feel safe with them. We know we can be who we really are when we are with people who love us or who have no power over us.

In order to live more fully in the present, we must learn how to feel safe even when a situation feels threatening to us. We must learn how to risk being vulnerable even when we can get seriously hurt, emotionally or physically. Does this not explain the appeal of "extreme" sports? When a person is climbing the side of a mountain with only a thin rope separating them from certain death, that person becomes very present. Is this not also what great athletes do in the last minutes of a championship game? They are vulnerable to the risk of disappointing their fans, yet they remain focused on doing what's important now for them, in order to get what they want in that moment—victory. They put out of their minds any fear of the consequences if they fail to perform. They feel safe within themselves, at least in that situation, knowing that they are doing the best they can regardless of what results occur. If they don't do this, then their self-doubt will most assuredly lead to a decline in their ability to perform with excellence.

Being capable of doing what's important now for you is a paradox. You must feel safe *especially* when a situation feels dangerous. Learning to be more present is therefore entirely about creating for yourself the ability to feel safe, *no matter what is happening around you*. You create this for yourself when you are able to seek fulfillment from within yourself, rather than searching for it from outside sources. When you feel fulfilled from within, you will feel good enough to make the mistakes that you will inevitably make when you dare to do what's important for you, right in the moment. When you are fully present, you are accepting of who you are. Your sense of self-worth is not linked to the world around you. Your every thought, feeling, and action is yours alone. In contrast, the thoughts, feelings, and actions of others are theirs alone. There is no such thing as blame, because they didn't "do it" to you, and you didn't "do it" to them. Life is happening and you are merely adapting to it. The journey hurts because you are giving up your desire to have power and influence over others. The rewards are sweet, however, because you are gaining power over yourself, the only person over whom any of us truly have control.

This separation of yourself from the world around you is not to be confused with building a wall around yourself and being insensitive to the feelings and needs of others. Indeed, the effect is quite the opposite. Because you are so open and vulnerable, you feel a tremendous compassion for those who are suffering. Yet you are aware at all times that their suffering is not your suffering. You are aware that it is not your duty to change, fix or alter their life experience, even if you think you "know" what's better for them more than they know themselves.

When you are present, you are not needy. You don't "need" others to change who they are or how they behave in order for you to feel safe or loved. You don't "need" positive or instant gratification in order to feel good about yourself. Your sense of love and well-being comes from within. If you feel unsafe, you trust that you will do what you need to do in order to feel at peace again.

To be present is to be living in a state of consciousness. You may do things out of habit, but nothing you do is an unconscious habit. Rather, you are very intentional. Every word, gesture, and deed is intentional. By the same token, you are highly conscious of what others say and do. Instead of being lost in your own thoughts, you are tuned in to the world around you. The result is that other people feel your "presentness" in a deep way. Paradoxically, you are much more connected to them because you are no longer reacting to them as if your sense of self-worth were affected by what they say or do to you. Because you feel complete, you can set your own needs aside and simply be present with them, giving them the love, empathy, or advice that are truly helpful to them. You don't act out of a need to feed your ego.

When you are present, you are tuned in to the four dimensions of your body, your mind, your heart, and your soul, all at once. You are aware of how you feel within your body. You are tuned in to your emotions. You are in charge of your thoughts, rather than having your thoughts race frenetically in your mind. You are also connected to your soul, that part of you that directs you towards some higher purpose for your life beyond the need for instant gratification. All this is happening for you at the same moment in time. You feel fully integrated. Your mind's eye sees what your physical eyes see. You feel energized and passionate about what you are doing. Your thoughts are focused on what is happening, and you adjust and adapt your actions accordingly in order to do what's right for you. Your soul resonates with a deep peace that you are living this moment as you were meant to live it.

When you are fully present, you become open to a new way of making decisions in your life, using your own "sixth sense". Your sixth sense is your "Inner Knowing", that part of you which is not logical or emotional. You seek to develop this part of you as your surest guide for knowing what's important now for you. You accept that this "knowing" is distinct and separate from thinking, which is merely logic and therefore only as good as the facts and skills that you possess. You understand that "knowing" is also not your feelings. Though your feelings may be powerful, they are merely your heart bringing the past back into the present. How can you be sure that your feelings about this present moment will bring about the same result as the last time? You cannot. Only your Inner Knowing rises above your thinking and your feeling. Learning how to recognize and act on your Inner Knowing is the greatest tool for discovering what's important now for you by living in the present.

THE YELLOW BRICK ROAD

The journey towards living more fully in the present is like traveling down a "yellow brick road", as Dorothy did in *The Wizard of Oz*. You must feel motivated by the idea that there is a Land of Oz, where you will truly feel happy with yourself and your life. You must feel willing to face many frightening obstacles along the way. You must do this knowing that you have no idea whether you will ever find this mystical place.

The Land of Oz is a state of mind in which you feel good about who you are, what you want, and how you do things. This is the place where you will no longer feel you need to improve in order to be a good-enough person. All your desires to make changes in your life will go away, to be replaced by a desire to know who you are and to be true to yourself. You will still be "improving", but your reason will have changed from trying to be good enough to wanting to fulfill your purpose in life.

For this journey to appeal to you, you must decide that this is a state of mind worth finding. Otherwise, the enormous barriers to getting there will most assuredly knock you off the path. The barriers are the many reasons why you don't *already* believe that you are good enough right now. Like the Lion, the Tin Man, and the Scarecrow, at the end of the journey you may discover that you *already* have the courage, the heart, and the intelligence to be good enough to do what's important now for you. This is precisely what makes this a frightening journey at times. You will find it terrifying to face the possibility that you tried so hard to be *better* than you are, when the "real you" was good enough all along.

When we try to be better than good enough, we erect walls around who we really are. We do this with the best of intentions. From infancy to adulthood, we learn from our parents, mentors, friends, and from life itself that we must be a certain kind of person if we are to be loved and successful. We might learn at age four, for example, that having temper tantrums results in our parents' being angry with us. So we learn to put up a wall around that part of us that wants to have temper tantrums. At the time we erect that wall, it serves us. But behind this wall, we are hiding part of who we really are, from others and from ourselves. In this way, our walls ultimately also make us blind to our "real" selves.

Removing a wall is very frightening. We erected that wall to protect ourselves from being hurt. We put it up in order to fit into how other people defined "good enough" for us. We learned that to have a temper tantrum might have painful consequences for us, such as rejection, criticism, humiliation, and attack. To tear down a wall is to expose ourselves once again to the risk of more pain and heartache.

Overcoming our innate desire to have that temper tantrum in the first place is the real secret to succeeding on this journey. When we have our walls up, we are *suppressing* who we are out of fear that our real selves might do something we'll regret. By facing our fears that we might actually do just that, we give ourselves the opportunity to *overcome* that dark side of our personalities. Then we can risk being who we really are without fearing that we will go on an angry rampage, or collapse in a weeping puddle of hopeless futility. Then we can truly dare to live in the present.

Facing each wall is frightening. That is why it is so vital to appreciate the rewards of being present. No sane person would otherwise want to go on this journey. Our fear of what might happen without that wall serves us. Our fear warns us that we are in danger. To then go ahead and do exactly what our fear is telling us *not* to do is...painful. If you are like me, at the moment of truth, you will want to bolt as fast as you can. Your memory of the rewards of being present is all that you will have to keep yourself from running away.

Each time you dare to cross through a doorway, you will likely experience powerful and bone-chilling emotions. If you consider acting in spite of your fear, the door will open for you, exposing a dark and foreboding abyss. You cannot see what is on the other side. You have to go forward with blind determination. You have to trust that you are not about to step off a cliff, hurtling towards a rocky and bloody bottom, like a skydiver whose parachute does not open. Each time you dare to break through a wall, you will be rewarded with the knowledge that you can live without that wall and survive to tell the tale. You will feel an unloading of a burden that you probably didn't even realize you had been carrying. The burden is your wall. The wall that you erected to protect yourself from being hurt unwittingly becomes a huge weight around your neck, aging you and crushing you. On the other side of each doorway, you will feel a deeper, more open connection to the people and the world around you. You will feel more connected with who you really are.

Crossing a doorway is not a one-time event. All it means is that the next time you stand at such a doorway, you will cross it with greater courage. Each subsequent doorway invites you to uncover your vulnerability at an ever-deeper level. In that respect, the doorways are tools for you. They are actions that you can take anytime you feel anxious, discontent, or worried about what is happening in your life and about what it might mean for you.

These are the six doorways that will help you shed your past and dare to do what the real you is aching for you to do:

1. **Listen to Your Body**: Facing the fear that your body is trying to tell you something that you do not want to know.
2. **Change Your Beliefs**: Facing the fear that what you have always believed to be true may not be so.
3. **Be Authentic**: Facing the fear of exposing to other people what you are truthfully thinking and feeling.
4. **Risk Disapproval**: Facing the fear of hurtful consequences once you allow others to see your true self.
5. **Let Go of Outcomes**: Facing the fear that you might crumble if your most valued people, possessions, and passions are taken away from you.
6. **Feel Your Feelings**: Facing the fear that you can no longer blame how you feel on other people.

By crossing through these six doorways with ever greater courage, you will begin to strip away the baggage of the past that is clouding your ability to *know* what's important now for you. Indeed, you will begin to build a wellspring of strength from within yourself that will allow you to withstand the enormous pressures you will undoubtedly feel from others around you as you begin to embrace the person you really are, rather than the one they wanted you to be. In doing so, you may not become rich, famous, or find your soul-mate, though any of these things might happen. But you will be more satisfied with who you are, with what you want, and with how you do what you are doing, regardless of what results you get for your efforts. You will feel the joy of being connected to the real you and to the world around you as it really is. You will know in your own heart that you are doing the best you can because you are focusing all of your body, mind, heart, and soul on what's important now for you. Is there anything more that you can ask of yourself?

Here are some closing thoughts about *The Journey*...

Remember...

- Keep a vision in your mind of a time when you were everything you wanted to be, letting it pull you forward when you feel defeated.
- Each of us is the best we can be when we are fully present, focused yet relaxed, curious yet non-judgmental, committed yet flexible.
- You will have the self-trust it takes to live fully in the present when you can create for yourself a deep sense of emotional safety, regardless of what is happening in your life.

Watch for...

- Pushing yourself too hard. You spent a lifetime building your inner walls of self-protection. You won't tear them all down in a month.

Try this...

- Start writing in a journal. Your self-disclosure will act like a mirror, helping you to see the real you that is hidden behind your walls. Do whatever you have to do in order to safeguard your journal so that you can frankly and openly write down your true thoughts and feelings.

Listen To Your Body

THE PAINS OF DENIAL

There is one undeniable truth about our body: it only exists in the present. Once an ache is over, it is gone. Sure, we *remember* how much we suffered. But that is a memory, not an actual pain. We can't feel yesterday's physical pain any more than we can feel tomorrow's pain. For that reason, our body is our most reliable barometer of what is happening inside ourselves in the present moment. When we learn how to read our body's messages, we acquire an invaluable tool that will teach us how to do what's important now in order to feel centered and present, capable of performing to the best of our ability.

Our body is constantly sending us signals. Our challenge is to listen. When we feel the urge to urinate, our body is talking to us. When we head for the nearest toilet, we are doing what's right for us. To not listen is to invite an embarrassing disaster. In that moment, what's important now is to respect what our body's needs are and to drop everything else we are doing, including our drawers! That sounds so easy, doesn't it? Yet, listening to our body is the doorway that many of us resist the most fiercely and for the longest time.

Ignoring your body's messages is so easy to do. You simply deny them. You rationalize them away. That ache? It will go away. That poor sleep? It's temporary while I finish this major project. That creaking joint? I'm just getting older. These plugged sinuses? It's the air quality in this town. That chest pain? It's...it's... I don't know what it is. I just wish it would go away.

Your body wants to tell you when something is wrong inside you. When you block out the message that your body is trying to send you, you are denying a truth within yourself that you don't want to know. You are pushing yourself to be someone or to do something that may not be right for who you really are. If you are like me, you might be afraid that if you listen to your body, you might have to make some changes in your life that are far more significant than merely going to the bathroom. This is the fear that makes crossing this doorway so frightening.

Our body is our first resource for learning the difference between what we *think* is important for us, and what we *know* is important for us. Our body sends us two types of signals. The first type is instant evidence of the fact that we are not entirely present. Our minds are disengaged. Our muscles are tense. Our jaws may be tightly clenched. We may even see "sunspots" or have blurry vision. We are "surviving" the moment. I call these body signals **"temporary frost"** because we are temporarily escaping the present.

The second type is **"permafrost"**. This is our body's way of telling us that we have not been doing what is important for us for a very long time. These are the mysterious aches and pains that seem to have no apparent cause. They are often attributed to prolonged periods of stress and anxiety. These are the ones that eventually thrust themselves in our faces, screaming "HEAR YE! HEAR YE! I AM NOT HAPPY. PLEASE PAY ATTENTION TO ME!"

These signals are your body's way of telling you that you may have stopped being true to who you really are. Perhaps you are trying to accomplish more than is right for you. Perhaps you are not speaking your truth on some important matters in your life. Maybe you feel frightened at some deep level that someone wants to hurt you, or even abandon you. No matter what the reason is, your body will always try to tell you when you are not fully present. Learning how to notice your body and what you can do about it is the first step in discovering how to live more fully in the present.

Let's first look at permafrost. Whether it's a headache, a sore back, aching joints, ringing in the ears, blood in one's stool, heart troubles, or any of a hundred other possibilities, our body begins to get our attention. Sooner or later, we cannot deny the existence of these pains. If you are like me, you will go to see a doctor. While you are on your way, you might want to ask yourself, what is my body trying to tell me? This is a difficult question. Our body doesn't send us an e-mail saying, "Bursitis in the shoulder! For relief, resolve your lingering resentment towards your spouse." Yet, that might be exactly what you need to do. Unresolved anger and negativity that is stored up inside your body surfaces in the form of ailments.

For example, a study reported in the April 15, 1999, edition of The Journal of the American Medical Association showed that 47 percent of arthritis and asthma patients demonstrated a clinical improvement in their condition after four months, by writing about the most stressful experience in their lives for twenty minutes a day for just three consecutive days. A comparison group that was asked to write about their daily plans showed that only 24 percent of its members experienced a clinical improvement. On two critical health dimensions, the asthma patients showed a 19 percent increase in lung function while the arthritis patients showed a 28 percent reduction in the severity of their disease. No improvements were found in the comparison group. When you resist looking at what inner wounds may be behind your outer aches, you also avoid doing what's important for you. The result, as the old saying goes, is that "If you just keep doing what you've been doing, you're going to keep getting what you've been getting." Or worse.

I would like to share with you some common permafrost ailments that I experienced long before I had heard of living in the present. My body sent my first clue in my right shoulder. I felt an unexpected, throbbing pain whenever I threw a baseball, swam the front crawl, or hit an overhand tennis serve. I could hardly lift my right arm after those kinds of activities. The idea that I could have an achy, arthritic joint at the tender age of thirty-two bothered me a lot. I was especially disturbed by the fact that this pain had come out of nowhere. Despite the best medical attention I could get, the only thing that relieved my pain was to not use the shoulder. Today, ten years later, I no longer have this pain. Not that I push it. But the pain is not there. Is it a coincidence that this pain has gone away, now that I am living a much happier, centered, and "present" life? Maybe. But I believe that my body was trying to tell me something and that when I "listened", my body healed itself.

My second clue came when I felt like I had a knife stabbed into my lungs. This pain stayed with me for several weeks. Thoughts of lung cancer kept popping into my mind, as I feared some kind of just retribution from my smoking days.

Perhaps that was just my guilty Catholic conscience at work. Nevertheless, the pain would not go away. I tried drugs, x-rays, and rest, without success. Finally, my wife Pam urged me to see my chiropractor. Reluctantly and skeptically, I agreed to go. When I explained my problem, the chiropractor gave me a knowing look and said, "Lay down on your back." With one huge push, he pressed down on my rib cage with his powerful hands. I yelped in pain like a stuck pig. A moment later, I felt fifty percent better. Two more visits, and I was as good as new. The chiropractor told me that he had often seen this symptom in his patients. I asked him to tell me what he believed to be the cause. His answer was blunt. "Stress." Apparently, the muscles around my rib cage had gone into an inflamed spasm from the enormous tension that I had felt in my chest.

Another major body signal for me was sinus congestion. My sinuses plugged up the day I moved to Oakville, a suburban town about thirty kilometers west of Toronto. My sinuses stayed that way for ten years. Early on, someone suggested to me that there were so many trees in Oakville that they affected the pollen count in the air, hence plugging my sinuses. I accepted this as a plausible explanation. Ten years and many changes to my life later, I still lived in that town but without the plugged sinuses. I can't tell you what you a delight it was to feel the phlegm release itself from my long-plugged sinus cavities, allowing me to breathe deeply and to better appreciate scents after so many years.

My diminishing memory also frightened me. I no longer remembered things like I used to. Of course, there were the usual tales of forgetting to pick up milk from the store on my way home or to do other errands. But what bothered me more was that I would wake up the morning after an evening of socializing with friends and struggle to remember what we had talked about. If I saw one of my friends a week later and they mentioned to me something that was discussed that evening, I would struggle to remember what was said. I would respond by saying, "Really? We talked about that? Oh yeah, sure, that's right. Let me get back to you." Then I would run to my wife, who would fill me in on my vague recall of the events of that night. This struck a nerve for me. Why was so little of what I was hearing sticking in my memory? I really wanted to know the answer to that question.

I even began to suffer from tinnitus. Tinnitus is a condition indicated by a continuous ringing sound in your ear. I felt like I had a high-pitched alarm going off inside my head, twenty-four hours a day. I went to see my doctor, who sent me to an ear specialist. The specialist examined my ear for any physical defects. He found none. He also put me through a battery of tests which required me to sit in a small booth where I was asked to listen for sounds and to indicate when I heard them. The results of the test were predictable. They concluded that there was nothing wrong with my ear or with my hearing, nor was there anything that could be done. Other people who had this problem told me that cutting out caffeine, salt, and sugar had dramatically helped them. I rarely used salt, and I had already eliminated caffeine. Eventually, my tinnitus cleared up on its own. In this case again, I believe that my symptoms vanished because I resolved so many of my past resentments and anxieties.

Serious health difficulties tend to show up in the weakest parts of our anatomy. In my case, that appears to be the colon. I've had several bouts of blood in my stool. Other members of my family suffer from colitis, a disease that inflames the colon. Colitis is known to be linked to stress. Indeed, each flare-up of my colon was correlated with periods of extreme stress in my life. When the stress went away, so did my symptoms of colitis.

A day finally arrived when my body hit me between the eyes like a sledgehammer. This was the point at which I could no longer deny the messages that my body was telling me. I had just returned from a stressful business trip to Europe. As vice-president of sales, I was responsible for hosting twenty-four of our best customers and their wives for nine days. Even though I had enjoyed a week's vacation after the business meetings, I came home feeling drained. I felt exhausted beyond anything I had ever felt before. The day after I returned, I tried to get up from the couch only to feel my head spin and to see the room go dark. I collapsed on the floor in the family room. With Pam's help, I staggered up to my bed. The instant I recovered consciousness, I felt filled with fear. Immediately, I tried to analyze what was wrong with me, but my brain and my whole body felt shut down. When I awoke eighteen groggy hours later, I admitted to myself for the first time that I was struggling. I knew that I had been pushing myself hard in my obsessive drive to "save the company" during the recession of the early 90s. I had been waking up at four o'clock in the morning for months, head racing with thoughts about work. Thinking was my passion, and now it was becoming hard work. Had I pushed too hard? The thought sent shivers down my spine. For the first time, I started questioning whether I was seriously harming myself. What if I permanently damaged my brain, preventing me from carrying on in my career? What if I was burning out? What if I didn't have what it takes to keep up the heavy pace that my career had demanded of me? These were possibilities that I did not want to consider. This time, however, my body got my attention, and I decided to listen to its messages.

My good friend and classmate whom I mentioned in the introduction to this book received a similar message from his body. He received it in the form of a serious heart attack at the age of thirty-six. That certainly got his attention—at least for awhile. He made major changes in his diet, even though he was only modestly overweight. He was not a smoker, but he hardly exercised. His father had also had heart problems, and I think my friend believed that most of his illness was genetic in origin, and therefore not in his control. Thus, he missed the most important problem—he did not change his outlook on work. He remained a driven workaholic. Within five years, he had another heart attack and died two weeks later. His death devastated me, leaving me feeling emotionally crushed. At forty-one, he left behind a shattered wife and two very young children.

Another friend of mine experienced the sad and unexpected loss of her forty-three-year-old husband. He died of a blood clot to the brain that was associated with lung cancer. He died within three months of the diagnosis, after having been in a state of depression for the previous year or so. My friend's doctor later told her that her husband's depression was likely caused by the onset of the cancer, which was probably hidden in his body for more than a year before it was discovered. She took a great deal of comfort from this observation. After all, she had watched him struggle over the last year of his life with low energy and a great deal of moodiness. Yet I wondered about the good doctor's observation. Did the cancer bring on the depression, or did the depression bring on the cancer? I think it would be rather hard to prove one way or the other. I have observed that people who get cancer at a younger age frequently have serious emotional difficulties in their lives.

I knew a woman who died of breast cancer at the age of fifty-three. She had been married for thirty years to a man who was difficult to live with. He was a perfectionist and a "control freak." He wanted things done his way and was not afraid to insist on it. He shamed and criticized his family without hesitation. As a result, nothing she ever did was good enough for him. Slowly, her self-esteem crumbled as she felt more and more inadequate as a human being. Despite this, she refused to leave the marriage. Those of us who knew her felt convinced that she willed herself to die. Whether it is true or not I will never know. I do not mention this to vilify her husband, either. Each of us is doing the best we can with what we know at a given time. That is just as true for this woman's husband as it was for her. Why he would want to dominate her, and why she was willing to be submissive to him, are really the questions that beg to be answered if we are to learn something useful from her life. For now, what matters is the notion that if you don't listen to your body, understand what it is trying to tell you, and then take corrective action, you are inviting serious risks to your physical health.

Alzheimer's is another disease that seems to be directly linked to unresolved emotional wounds. My mother has been diagnosed as being in the early stages of Alzheimer's Disease. Ironically, this is a disease which renders patients incapable of living in the present. They are irresistibly drawn to relive scenes and events from the past, leaving them unable to remember what happened just a few minutes earlier.

Some people stubbornly refuse to listen to their bodies. Some have nervous breakdowns. Some have heart attacks. Some get cancer. Some die. All of us can deny to ourselves what is often patently obvious to those around us. If this has happened to you or to someone you love, just remember that each of us is always doing the best we can with what we know at a given time, even if it seems wrong in retrospect.

COPING

The problem with listening to your body is that you might act on the message. Then you have to wake up the next morning and face what you did. I think that is why this doorway is the hardest one of all to cross. Many of us get comfortable in the predictable routines of our lives. We know what route we'll be driving, what people we'll be working with, and how much pay we'll be taking home. We know whom we'll be coming home to and whom we'll be going to the party with. Taking action by listening to your body can throw a wrench in all that, leaving you with no idea what you'll do, or how you'll earn a living, or whether you'll ever be happy again.

A year after my collapse on the floor in the family room, I quit my job. I survived that year by beginning to do what I call Coping. Coping is where you do things that help you relieve the physical symptoms that your body is sending your way. I reduced my work hours. I increased my commitment to exercise. I quit drinking caffeinated beverages such as coffee and cola. I also negotiated a healthy severance package from my company, leaving me in good financial shape and thus able to take on the risk of being unemployed. I felt scared even as I felt optimistic that maybe a little time off would have me feeling as good as new again.

Four months later, having had a two-week vacation and having restricted my work time to a couple of days a week doing some consulting, I felt as poorly as ever. I felt tired and low in energy, with poor sleep habits and a general feeling of malaise. I decided to take a full month off to roller-blade, exercise, and relax in order to really get myself back into top shape. To my chagrin, that also did nothing for me. My head felt heavy. Concentrating was a burden. I could not understand why I felt the way I did. I was physically healthy. I was highly employable with a stellar career track record. My wife was working full-time in a highly paid job. I should have had the world by the tail. Instead, I was wilting and getting more scared by the day.

That was when I began to seriously increase my coping. Like fighting a cold by taking pills, coping doesn't cure the underlying cause of not being present. Rather, it reduces the symptoms and the suffering. Coping is a pretty good place to start. There are dozens of ways to cope. Diet, exercise, and time management are three of the most popular and effective ones. Other terrific methods are relaxation techniques like yoga, tai chi, meditation, stretching, deep breathing, and vocal chord relaxation. Spa-like treatments such as massages, facials, reflexology (foot massage), and Reiki treatments (hands-on touching) are also wonderful ways to temporarily feel present, balanced, and reconnected to your body.

I have tried most of the popular methods. Some worked better for me than others. I investigated my diet. I was shocked at how little I knew about the fat content of the foods I was eating. I switched to a low-fat diet and lost ten pounds in six weeks. I looked much better, but I still felt awful.

Exercise worked well for me—I had already been doing it for several years. A twenty-minute workout on a stair-climbing machine at the beginning of the day was like putting jet fuel into my body for at least half a day. In a different way, lifting weights also helped me to cope. There was something about pushing for those last two repetitions that reconnected my racing mind to the faint awareness that I even had a body.

Time management is a wonderfully important coping skill. I am not just talking about making lists and identifying priorities. These are crucial, basic skills. But good time management is also about knowing how to delegate tasks and coaching others on how to do tasks that really don't belong to you in the first place. Good time management can take you a long way towards handling ever increasing workloads without feeling that you're drowning.

One of my enduring favorite ways of coping is meditation. I use the Transcendental Meditation method. Twice a day, I sit quietly for twenty minutes while silently repeating a mantra in my mind. A mantra is a single sound or a word with no meaning that is repeated to help you calm your mind. I meditated on a commuter train for a number of years. Other effective methods include listening to visualization tapes, praying, and repetitive chanting and singing. When I emerge from a good meditation, I feel like I am seeing the world anew. I notice the trees and the sky, I smell the grass, I truly "see" the unfamiliar people walking by me. Meditation has the delightful effect of emptying the mind of all thoughts. When that happens, you are able to be fully present, at least for a few minutes. I don't believe that it's a coincidence that the answers to difficult questions about what's right for me will then suddenly pop into my mind.

I cannot overstate the importance of good sleep to living in the present. I find that first thing in the morning, before my brain has had a chance to get engaged, I often feel a sudden clarity about what's important for me to be doing about some pressing question. These are moments when I feel especially present and at peace. Ironically, the quality of our sleep often feels like it is out of our control. Like being happy, good sleep is a side effect of living a balanced life in which we feel good about ourselves.

Anxiety, worry, and resentment cause poor sleep, which in turn makes being present all that much more difficult. These conditions feed each other in a vicious cycle that leads to "permafrost". In the long run, when you are true to yourself, you will sleep more soundly as a byproduct of your efforts. In the short run, you can pay attention to those factors that aggravate your inability to sleep. If I eat spicy foods or if I eat late at night, my sleep is much poorer. If I push my brain to do heavy-duty thinking late into the evening, I wake up early and I do not feel rested. If I drink alcohol or caffeine when I feel tension and stress in my body, my sleep is negatively affected. These and many other factors are within your control if you want to get that vital gift—a good night's sleep.

Sometimes we choose unhealthy ways to cope. Excessive drinking, smoking, working, eating, gambling, and substance abuse are examples of unhealthy ways. These are ways to "numb out" so that we don't feel the message that our body is sending to us. When we numb out, we are not present. Understanding why we want to do that to ourselves is a lesson that each of us must face in our journey towards discovering what's important for us. For me, it turned out that "de Nile" was not just the name of a river. I just did not want to hear what my body was trying so hard to tell me.

All of these coping techniques have one thing in common. They are temporary. When my low-fat diet did not improve my mental state, I decided to see a stress counselor for the first time in my life. It was then that I truly opened the door to understanding why I was having those anxious thoughts and feelings in the first place, and to then taking action to overcome them.

Coping skills are crucial to our ability to survive anxiety and unhappiness. If you feel stuck in that way, your body may be sending you messages even now. If you are as fortunate as I was, the message will be clear for you without having seriously damaged your long-term health. You may decide to listen to your body and act. If you do, I encourage you to remember a key message of this book: You are always doing what's important now for you, even if it seems illogical, unhealthy, and even self-destructive. The result is that you will feel anxious and even fearful from time to time. When that happens, your coping skills will help you to regain your sense of balance and perspective, so that you can make a new decision in this new moment.

TEMPORARY FROST

As you try to live more fully in the present, you will begin to notice the more subtle signs of what is happening within your body, right in the moment. Four years after seeing my first stress counselor, I met another therapist who would profoundly influence me. His name was Dr. André Stein, and he taught me to appreciate the powerful signals that our body sends us in the moment. These are the signs that I call "temporary frost," when we are numbing out from physical or emotional pains that are happening in a specific moment.

At sixty, André was a fit man, married to a woman seventeen years younger than himself, and the proud father of five children. André was sixty going on forty. He had recently retired from the University of Toronto after a twenty-seven-year tenure as a psychology professor, in order to practice psychotherapy full-time, in addition to writing a fifth book. As a Jewish child survivor of the Nazi death camps during World War II, he had a lot more than just academic experience to draw on. I was always amazed at how present he was with me during our sessions. Nothing escaped his attentive eyes and ears. He remembered every relevant detail of our conversations without ever taking a note.

André loved to observe my body language while we were talking. If I was approaching a deep, emotional pain from my past, he would notice my breathing become very shallow, my arms fold up tightly, my shoulders hunch over, my legs cross tightly and my voice grow monotone and lifeless. He would ask me what I was feeling in those moments. I always had the same answer, "Not much. Numb, I guess." I came to realize that these were powerful signs to indicate that I was avoiding being present with my own reality in that moment.

When we are temporarily not present, we are checking out. At some level, we are wishing we were somewhere else. Our minds are disconnected from our emotions and even from our body. Perhaps my first hint at how often I did this should have come when I broke my leg in Mexico four years before my collapse in the family room. My wife and I had just finished lunch. I had a drink in my hand, the first drink of the afternoon—a banana daiquiri. As I walked from the bar towards our chairs, part of my mind took notice of some kids playing with a ball in the pool. The other part of my mind was in its usual place—racing with thoughts. As I kept walking, I bumped into a table that stood in my path. Without looking at it, I stepped to the left around the table while continuing to look at the kids in the pool to my right. The patio instantly disappeared from under my feet. In a microsecond, I felt my sandal hook onto something, followed by a loud crack. I hit the beach, slumped onto my side and cried out in pain, "I broke my leg! I broke my leg!" I had snapped both bones above my right ankle. If only I had been present! Then I might have noticed the danger. Instead, I had been inattentive, which caused me to become more accident-prone.

Staring, shallow breathing, tension in one's body, especially around the eyes, temples, and jaw, and a vibrating voice are a few of the signals that our body sends to let us know that in this moment, we are not fully present. Cold hands and feet, sexual dysfunction, constipation, stomach churning, and avoiding eye contact are other ways in which we can recognize that there is something happening in the present over which we feel tense and uncomfortable. Even nervous habits such as nail-biting and picking at our skin, eyes, ears, or hair are visible evidence of our discomfort in the present moment.

They are the signs that we are feeling pressure of some kind. Who we are, what we want, or what we are doing is, for some reason, not good enough in that moment. In ways that we will explore in more depth later on, we feel in danger. Our body is trying to tell us that this is our truth. Our challenge is to notice it, and to do what's right for us in that moment. Each of the six doorways in this book are actions that will serve you to discover how to feel safe enough to do what's important for you when things seem wrong.

Part of my personal journey included leaving my wife and getting a divorce. Immediately after we separated, my body spoke to me about how I did not feel sexually safe with other women. I was dating another woman when, to my great annoyance, I had difficulty having orgasms with her—not difficulty with erections, just with orgasms. No matter what I did, it was like my "trigger" was no longer functioning. This had never happened in all the years that I had been with my wife. I felt angry at myself. "What the hell is going on with my stupid body?" I could feel my adrenaline shoot up as I beat myself up because my body was failing to perform as it was "supposed to."

I spoke to André about my anger and frustration over this. He said, "The French have a name for orgasm. They call it "le petit mort"—the little death. In order to reach orgasm, you have to let go, just as you do in dying. For some reason, you must not feel safe enough to "let go" with the person that you are with." He was right. I became aware of the fact that my brain would notice when I was getting close to orgasm. Instead of letting go and going with it, the thought itself would involuntarily numb out any feeling I was having. The more I tried to not think about it, the worse it got. This was the strangest yet strongest evidence I experienced of how not being present negatively affected my body's ability to perform at its best. Being present means feeling safe enough to let go of control and thereby to stop having fearful or anxious thoughts.

Understanding what you are fearing in a given moment, and then overcoming it, is the challenge that must be faced in order to live more fully in the present. Initially, your challenge is to become present to your body's aches and pains, and to become willing to consider what they mean for you. Then you become open to the possibility that you may have been living your life in a way that is not true to who you really are. That in itself is an enormous achievement. You may discover that you don't need to make any great changes. But the fact that you are willing to honestly consider them opens your mind to discovering what's important now for you, no matter what you *wish* were happening.

LOVING YOUR BODY

When someone sees your body, are you comfortable with what they see? Are you at peace with your body's inadequacies and shortcomings? Many of us are not. Many of us wish we had bodies with a better shape, straighter teeth, smoother skin, and more abilities, to name just a few of the qualities that we ascribe to a "good enough" body. Accepting your body is an important cornerstone for feeling safe enough to live in the present and thereby to know what's important for you to say or do in a given situation.

I once took a course in which the instructor asked us, "What is the purpose of your body?" My instinctive response was, "To carry my brain around!" What a revelation that was for me! I had so little respect for my body. In many ways, I even hated my body. I saw every shortcoming of my body as proof of my inadequacy. My teeth were too big. My legs could not run fast enough. My surgically-repaired left knee could no longer take the pounding of aggressive downhill skiing. I had no hair on my chest. My shoulder, wrist, and hip ached regularly. I felt annoyed and embarrassed at these shortcomings.

When I thought about my body as a child, I remembered a much deeper anger. I was a terrible grade-school athlete. I could not outrun, out-fight, or out-jump anyone. I was ugly, with big teeth, pigeon toes, and ears that stuck out. How the neighborhood kids had teased me about my body's faults! In high school, I was one of the very last boys to reach puberty. I cursed my body during my first two years of high school. All the other guys could shave, but I was still covered in peach fuzz. "Why me?" I cried out in angry self-disgust.

When I reached my late teens and early twenties, all that changed. I paid a great deal of attention to my body, but in a superficial way. Getting a tan every summer was a top priority for me. I let the sun bleach my hair to a nice, blond color. One summer, I worked on a sod farm, and my arms grew tremendously in strength. The girls noticed the ripples. The guys noticed that I could hit a baseball over the outfield fence for the first time. At twenty, I was loving my body. My body was how I attracted women and impressed my friends with my athletic abilities.

Our bodies are an important factor in our ability to feel good enough to live in the present. André once enlightened me as to why beautiful movie stars such as Marilyn Monroe committed suicide in their forties. Their self-worth was entirely anchored in their physical selves. Once their physical selves began to deteriorate through age, they needed to find a new anchor in their emotional, mental, or spiritual selves. If they did not, they felt worthless and afraid of being rejected and abandoned. In their own self-perception, they were no longer good enough to even deserve to live.

When I realized how little I loved my body, I decided that I wanted to change that. How could I live in the present while wishing that my body were different from what it really was? Do you feel that way about your body? Before you can change your attitude about your body, you have to understand it. As mature adults, many of us don't actually hate our body. Rather, we just ignore it. We notice it only if we feel discomfort somewhere. Then we become angry with the body. We expect it to be there, ready to look good and to perform well, without fail. We take our body for granted.

While our physical self was an extremely important anchor for us as young adults, it can become increasingly irrelevant when we reach mature adulthood. This is especially true for those of us who become highly career-focused. Our self-worth becomes anchored in a new dimension—our minds. Our success comes from how smart and clever we are.

Our self-worth is always anchored in one or more of the four dimensions of our human being—our physical, mental, emotional, or spiritual selves. In addition to the body and the mind, many people depend on their emotions for their self-worth anchor. They rely on their ability to influence others by being likeable or even tough and scary so that they will get what they want. Others rely on their soul, their sense of destiny and purpose in order to feel good about what they are doing. As you read this book, it will be helpful for you to regularly consider *which* self-worth anchor you are leaning upon in order to decide what is important for you in a given moment. This alone will give you great insight as to *why* you decide what's important now for you, even if it is sometimes ineffective or even harmful to you, such as when you are overly cautious, overly-aggressive, or are over-doing activities like work, sports, sexual fantasizing or "busy-tasks."

You must learn to love your body if you are to feel safe enough to live in the present. When you are aware that someone might see rolls of fat around your waist, unwanted hair on your body, blotches on your skin, crooked teeth in your mouth, or stretch marks on your tummy, your mind becomes preoccupied with what someone might think if they saw those "inadequate" parts of yourself. At that moment, you are no longer able to be present. You are self-conscious and anxious, even if only mildly.

When you embrace your body the way it really is, you pay attention to its well-being. You rest if you feel you need a rest. You notice what food or drink your body seems to require in this particular moment. You appreciate what your body *does* do for you. You stop beating yourself up for its inadequacies. My first step towards doing this came when I felt thankful for the baby boy that my body helped to conceive. That one miracle alone helped me to forgive the many other shortcomings that I felt about my body. I do not want to mislead you that I waved a magical wand and suddenly loved my body. I had to cross many doorways to get there. I had numerous beliefs and expectations about my body that caused me to disrespect it. I needed to heal many emotional wounds before I could truly embrace my physical self.

Our body is a phenomenal gift. More than any other aspect of our humanness, it is what tells us that we are alive in this moment. I encourage you to commit yourself to accepting your body as it is today.

Here are some closing thoughts on *Listen to Your Body*...

Remember...
- We deny what our aches and pains might mean because it serves us to do so. Our fear is that we might have to make unwanted changes in our lives.
- Whether your heart pounds or your voice quivers, your body is telling you that you do not feel safe. For reasons you may not yet understand, you do not feel good enough to handle the present moment, thereby limiting your ability to know and do what's important now for you.
- When you heal your inner wounds, you give your body the fullest opportunity to heal your physical ailments, too.
- One of your four human dimensions—body, mind, heart, or soul, will largely anchor your self-worth and unconsciously influence what's important now for you.

Watch for...
- Aches and pains that have no apparent cause. Is there a pattern of situations that helps to explain when the pains appear and disappear?
- Numbing out your body's messages with drugs, alcohol, over-work, smoking, gambling, or other negative coping tools.

Try this...
- Get to know your body's "language". Notice how your body reacts when you are under pressure. How is that stopping you from doing what's important for you in that moment?

- Experiment with various coping techniques to see which ones help you feel relaxed, loose, and present.

As Winston Churchill once put it, "This is not the end. Nor is it the beginning of the end. But perhaps it is the end of the beginning." The end of the beginning will arrive for you when you get tired of coping. Like running on a tread mill, coping is a way to keep doing what you're doing without collapsing. If you want to actually *eliminate* the stress and tension that is blocking you from feeling clear and confident about what's important now for you, you can consider crossing a new doorway—changing how you perceive what's happening in your life, without changing your life itself.

Change **2** Your Beliefs

BELIEFS DEFINE OUR REALITY

Y ou cannot do what's important for you if your mind cannot accept what is happening in *this* present moment. If you react like a deer frozen in the headlights of an oncoming car, your fate may well end up being the same as the deer's—to be run over by the velocity of real life. My neighbor told me a story about an incident in which his ability to be present saved his life. He was driving his car, waiting third in line to make a left-hand turn at a busy highway intersection. Suddenly, he noticed a large tanker truck coming towards the intersection from his left. The truck was moving very quickly, too quickly to be able to stop for the red light. In order to avert disaster, the truck driver veered hard to his right, heading directly towards my neighbor and the two cars in front of him. Without a second's hesitation, my neighbor leaped towards the passenger door, flung open the door and tossed himself out of his car, rolling out into the middle of the road. A split second later, he heard a massive crash and then felt a shower of broken glass and liquid all over his body. When he looked up, the tanker truck had rolled over and crushed all three cars, including his. The drivers of the first two cars were killed instantly.

In some situations, your ability to be present could make the difference between life and death. When you are fully present in those situations, your mind, body, heart, and soul know exactly what's important now for you. You do not need to think about it, check your feelings, or ponder your options. You know and you act. That same extraordinary sense of awareness can work for you in any moment, not just in moments of crisis. This is the ability that lets you say and do the right thing at the right time, rather than wishing, after the fact, that you had thought of that great comeback line or made that brilliant move.

Doing what's important now comes from having the extraordinary ability to know what's right for you in response to whatever life is throwing at you. In order to be present to such a degree, you must develop your ability to accept what is happening and to adapt instantly to what it means for you, without undue analytical thought. This ability will come from becoming conscious of your beliefs. If you have an old belief that transport trucks don't make unexpected right-hand turns and crush bystanding cars, you will find it difficult to believe what your eyes are seeing. You will risk being like the proverbial deer, frozen in the headlights of impending disaster. When you become aware of your beliefs, you can change them or let go of them instantly if necessary. This can be a frightening doorway to cross. You must face the fear that what you have always believed to be true may, in fact, not be so.

We learn our beliefs from the school of life. If we tasted honey as a young child and discovered that it was good, we acquired a belief: *Honey should taste good*. If we were repeatedly spanked for having temper tantrums, we may have acquired a belief: *Showing our feelings is dangerous*. If our parents noticed only our misbehavior and ignored us the rest of the time, we may have acquired a belief: *I am a bad person*. Throughout the course of our lives, we acquire thousands of beliefs. These beliefs form an unwritten and unconscious "rule book of life" for each of us, based on our past experiences.

Beliefs are what tell us *how* we will get what we want in any given moment. We use them to interpret and to make sense of every event that happens around us. If a person was stung by a bee as a young child, she may have acquired a belief: *"Stay away from bees, or you'll get hurt."* The fact that she has this belief will become evident by how she reacts to the presence of a bumblebee buzzing about her head. If she feels panicky, swings her arms at the bumblebee, and runs away, she can be sure that she has this sort of belief. If she feels calm and doesn't move, she probably has a different belief: *"If I stay calm, the bee will go away without stinging me."* Is either belief the "right one"? No. She could run and still get stung. She could stay calm and still get stung. Her belief reflects her experience. Nothing more. Nothing less. Once a person has created a belief, it sinks deeply into their unconscious mind, ready to serve them at a moment's notice, should a similar situation come up.

Once you discover that every thought and feeling you have is colored by your beliefs, you open the doorway to taking charge of your life. You become aware that instead of changing your job, your spouse, or your neighborhood, you can change how you feel about each one by changing your beliefs. By changing some of my deeply-held beliefs, I grew capable of ridding myself of many of my "frozen-in-the-head-light" type of reactions to life's unexpected tanker trucks. Discovering that the process was quite simple is what makes this a scary doorway to cross. To think that I had that much power over myself was exhilarating, even as it was frightening to think that I had suffered needlessly for all that time.

The main problem with our beliefs is that we are not consciously aware of them. They just kick in, and we act on them in the same way that a wild animal acts on its instincts without thought. They drive our feelings and motivate us to worry and fret. They affect our ability to see and hear what another person is actually saying. We are so uncomfortable with beliefs that are different from ours that we tend to automatically filter out people, events, and situations that don't fit with what we believe. The result is that our beliefs distort our perception of the present. You can see this when someone begins talking about something controversial during dinner. We tend to tune out or try to change the subject. You can also observe this when someone goes into panic mode, like the child who is afraid of bees. Their beliefs are blocking them from seeing and hearing what is actually happening. They are unable to risk doing something new, even though this might be a much wiser choice, such as standing perfectly still until the bee goes away.

Yet, imagine how difficult life would be if we did not have beliefs. There are benefits to having beliefs. What if you came upon a set of stairs and you had no beliefs about staircase safety? You would feel compelled to examine the staircase step by step to verify that it could hold your weight. Otherwise, how could you know that it wouldn't just collapse when you stepped on it? Thankfully, the many times that you have stepped on a staircase before, it did not fall down. So you decide to believe that stairs are safe and you walk on them. In this example, the past is a safe predictor of the future. This is true in hundreds of other situations that we each come across every day, from believing that we will enjoy going to the beach, to believing that oysters taste wonderful. (Well, I believe that they do!)

However, the past is not always an accurate predictor of the future. As a result, our beliefs are an enormous barrier to doing what's important for us in the present moment. Sometimes, what was true in the past is simply no longer true now. The fact that your boss assigns you to a "special project," and the last two people who were given the same assignment were both fired does not mean that the same thing will happen to you. If the traffic unexpectedly begins to back up in the same way it did yesterday, this does not mean that it will *stay* backed up today. It might, but it also might not. The past does not equal the future. Even if your fears turn out to be true, this does not necessarily mean that tragedy is coming your way. Events are only scary if you believe them to be so. If you believe that getting fired is bad, then it is bad. But I have seen many people who were fired go on to much bigger and better things in their working lives.

Each of us has hundreds of such beliefs. I was amazed to discover some of the beliefs that I held—beliefs that I did not know even existed! Many of them showed up when I first got married. I would arrive home from work around seven o'clock, just as I had during the previous six years of my working life. My wife would get home from her job around five o'clock. Within a few weeks, she began to object to what she perceived to be my late working hours. I looked at her with astonishment. As I had grown up on a farm and had held various summer farm jobs, my working day had never ended sooner than at six o'clock. Working to that hour was my habit. Leaving my job sooner had never even *occurred* to me!

My wife had different beliefs. Her father had always come home from work by five o'clock. Working later than five o'clock hadn't occurred to her either! And so we encountered the first of many conflicts in that first year of our marriage around our beliefs. Mine was *"Good workers work long hours."* Hers was, *"Good husbands come home in time to have dinner with their family."* Who was right? Neither of us was. We each had a belief that served us. Even more important, we each wanted the other person to buy into our belief. I wanted her to believe that I *had* to work long hours. She wanted me to believe that good husbands come home in time for dinner.

Conflict with others is one of the best ways to notice your beliefs. Conflict comes from the difference in beliefs between people. That is why changing a belief is such a powerful way to feel safe enough to be more present. If you don't like a conflict that is causing you stress and unhappiness, you don't need to convince the other person to give in or to change. You can merely change yourself! You can eliminate the conflict by changing your belief. Of course, most of us would rather see the other person change their belief, while we cling to ours. That's part of what makes this a scary doorway to cross.

Eventually, my wife accepted my belief that I "had" to work long hours, which ended that particular conflict. Of course, that would only be true if she really changed her belief. Perhaps she just swallowed hard and resentfully tolerated my late working hours. Then she would have harbored some undertone of anger towards me about this. Resentfully tolerating someone else's belief is not the same as changing your belief. That is sweeping your truth under the carpet and not being true to yourself. You will know the truth of this the next time a similar situation arises. If you feel angry or resentful, you can be sure that you did not change your belief about what that other person should be saying or doing.

You created your beliefs based on the experiences and the knowledge that you acquired in your past life. When you get close to a particular belief, you will often remember the exact moment that you acquired it. I remember that when I was eight years old, a man was visiting my father. I did not like this guy. I just had a bad feeling about him. He seemed mean to me. Well, a few minutes later, this man decided to tease me about my hair. Then he reached over and pulled the short hairs in front of my ears. I yelped in pain. I felt so angry at him. My father just stood there and did nothing, as if this were just some kind of joke. I was angry at my father, too, for letting this guy do what he did to me. I remember acquiring a belief that day, *"When I grow up, I will never ever rely on anyone else. I will look after myself by myself!"* Oh, what conviction I felt that day for my belief to become totally self-reliant!

Therein lies the problem with beliefs. A belief that made perfect sense to us as an eight-year-old becomes ingrained in our unconscious mind for life. In my case, what worked for me as an eight-year-old was no longer working for me at the age of thirty-eight. I had a hard time letting anyone get close to me emotionally all of my life. I am sure that the belief that I formed that day was one reason. I developed a deep-seated distrust of other people. In order to keep people out, I had built a wall of which I was not even consciously aware during my adult life. This wall dramatically hindered my ability to develop and maintain close relationships. I was simply too afraid of people, based on a variety of beliefs that I held about myself and about what people might do to me if I were truly open and vulnerable.

Our beliefs play out in our lives like an unseen subtext, always there, yet never visible. Uncovering your beliefs is like wiping the steam off the bathroom mirror after taking a shower. You can see yourself more clearly, but not perfectly clearly. I once had an instructor who explained that seeing our beliefs was like looking at the underside of a hand-woven carpet. While the top side looks beautiful, the under-side is a big, tangled mess, until you begin to examine each knot one by one. Then you can see how the knots fall into place and result in the work of art that is visible to the out-side world.

Beliefs are not to be trifled with. People kill for their beliefs, as is evident in the wars that mankind has wrought upon itself. People get suicidal for their beliefs, as we saw in the stock market crash of 1929, when people jumped out of windows after they had lost their fortune. People worry and fret and regret for their beliefs. Beliefs compel us to react to the events in our lives in a way that frequently seems com-pletely out of our control. If we get angry at someone because they are late, for example, most of us do not think for a moment that we are causing our own anger. We are convinced that it was *their* behavior that made us feel angry, not our belief that *"responsible people show up on time."* Or perhaps an even more deep-seated belief, *"I deserve to be treated better than that."*

The idea that we are responsible for our own feelings based on our beliefs makes crossing this doorway frighten-ing. We must acknowledge the possibility that we can no longer blame another person for how we are feeling. In fact, we can actually change *in this very moment* how we experi-ence the same event that drove us crazy just minutes earlier! This concept was so enormous that it took me a few years to fully grasp and own it as truth. In the beginning, what matters is that changing your beliefs is a wonderful opportunity to come to peace about many things in your past that you cannot change anyway.

OWNING YOUR BELIEFS

As I mentioned in the prologue of this book, the secret to knowing what's important now for you is to be fully present with yourself. A crucial part of accomplishing this is to own your beliefs as separate from the beliefs of other people. We each have lived a life that is unique and distinct from the life of another. Even close siblings who live in the same family and in the same environment experience the events in their lives very distinctly. Therefore, it only makes sense that each of us has our own unique set of beliefs.

You can recognize the truth of this by seeing how different people react to the exact same situation. If a beautiful woman walked into a room full of different people of different cultures, ages, and genders, and removed her blouse to reveal her naked breasts, would every person in the room experience the same reaction? Not likely. An older woman might find herself feeling disgust. A younger woman might admire the bare-breasted woman's bravado. A young man might instantly feel lust and desire. Another man might feel intimidated. Some people might feel angry and want to see the woman punished. The possible reactions are limitless, even though every person in the room saw the exact same thing. Each person's reaction must therefore be about their beliefs regarding women going topless in a public place.

The great irony of this is that many of us believe that the opposite *should* be true. We expect others to see things the way we do, just as I had expectations of my wife and of her views about my working late. When others don't see things the way we do, we tend to judge the situation in one of two ways: Something is wrong with them, or, something is wrong with me. If we think that something is wrong with us, we begin to judge ourselves. "What is wrong with me? Why am I so insensitive to her feelings? The least I can do is come home early enough to eat dinner with her." If we think that something is wrong with the other person, we use our beliefs to begin to judge them instead. "What kind of a woman doesn't understand that my job demands long working hours?"

We are not able to be present when we are judging. Our minds become filled with critical thoughts, leaving us close-minded to what is happening in the present moment. Overcoming this enormous mind clutter is what much of this book is about. To be present is to let go of our beliefs about what each of us "should" be doing according to our own "rules of life." Only then are we able to be curious, open, and adaptive to doing what's right for us in this new moment. We can accept that what is happening is not a reflection of whether we are "good enough," or whether anyone *else* is good enough. It's just what is happening, leaving us with the same question every time: "What's important now for me, in this new moment?" This question opens us up to making wise choices and to performing to the best of our abilities.

The first step towards this ideal state of mind is to own your beliefs as separate and distinct from those of other people. You must accept that just because you believe something to be true, this does not make it the truth for anyone else. If you believe that the dishes can stay in the sink for days, this does not make that true for your spouse. If you believe that people *should* show up on time for appointments, this does not mean they also believe that. If you believe that abortion or capital punishment are wrong, well, others are entitled to have different beliefs, ones which are not in your control to change.

We frequently encounter situations that contradict our beliefs. Whether it is our spouse's odd habits, or the way our boss wants us to do our job, we notice that what's happening isn't what we wish were happening. In those moments, our emotions get stirred or "triggered." Beliefs are the buttons that ignite our emotional fires. They are the "filter" through which we evaluate every moment, checking to see if we are safe or unsafe, and therefore what we or others "should" be doing in this present moment. Once we filter an event through our belief system, we will have an emotional reaction that happens in a microsecond. This amazing phenomenon works like this:

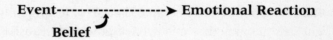

Event----------------------➤ **Emotional Reaction**
                    Belief

The truth of this only becomes evident when you slow your mind down enough to be able to see it. I was shocked at how often this was happening to me each and every day. When someone cuts me off in traffic, that is an event. With the beliefs that I held about bad drivers, I would instantly feel annoyed. I wanted to curse the other driver, give him a dirty look, or do something else out of anger! In the microsecond between the event (getting cut off) and my reaction (anger), my brain filtered that event through my belief system. My beliefs were something like, *"Good drivers don't cut off other drivers."* And, *"Bad drivers deserve to be punished."*

Beliefs sound rather strange when you say them. But the emotions that are stirred up when you react are a sure-footed guide that will tell you whether you have bumped into a belief. At that moment, your belief is causing you to have an emotional reaction. You are mad, sad, afraid, or glad because the event either clashes or fits with your belief system. The hard part of this is accepting that, by default, your unhappiness must not be the result of the event; it must be caused by your own belief—remember the example of those observing the topless woman.

When you accept that each of us has a unique set of beliefs, you open yourself to the possibility that the reactions of others to your actions are not about you. Their reactions are about *them* and their beliefs! If you are entitled to your beliefs and your emotional reactions, then perhaps you can accept that others are entitled to their beliefs and their reactions also. How liberating that realization was for me! No longer did I automatically see that there was something wrong with others *or* with me if I reacted differently to the same situation. Then I became capable of feeling fully present in situations that might have previously caused me to feel tense and anxious. Instead, I felt clear-minded and capable of discerning what was important for me to do, regardless of my past beliefs or their beliefs.

Ultimately, the foundation to living fully in the present is to separate your beliefs from the beliefs of others. You can do this with a new belief:

"It's not about me."

No matter what someone is doing or how someone is reacting to you or to a given situation, it's not about you. They are simply feeling emotions and behaving in accordance with their own beliefs. The idea that "It is not about me" is quite radical. If you adopt this view, you can be sure that some people will not like this new belief in you. They *want* you to react to their hurts and angers. They *want* you to feel that it is your fault and that you *made* them feel angry, or scared, or sad. But it is not true. They are choosing to feel that way based on their belief system.

What *is* true is that your behavior triggered them. That is the part for which you must take responsibility. "Yes, I said, 'You never help out in the kitchen.'" I find it helpful to validate that you have heard and understood how they feel. "I understand that you feel angry because I said that you never help out in the kitchen." You must feel the truth of their pain. You must feel compassion for that person, even as you let them own their own feelings all to themselves. Mirroring what they've said and empathizing with their feelings does not mean that you *made* them have those feelings. You are taking responsibility for what you *did*, but not for how they *feel*.

Another instructor of mine once described the world as a "beliefs market place." She said that we spend each day of our lives buying and selling beliefs to each other. Trying to make others feel responsible for our feelings is one way we have of "selling" our beliefs to others, hoping that we can influence them to change their behavior so that we'll feel better. My first wife and I did this to each other all the time. The biggest sell-job that we did to each other was the belief that we were responsible for each other's happiness. I often felt like I was a "bad husband," because I did not live up to her beliefs about what constituted "good husband" behavior, whether it was cleaning up the dishes after dinner on a timely basis or picking out an acceptable birthday gift. I did the same to her when I would give her a little dig if she did not pay enough attention to me or if she spent too much money on clothes.

When we understand how our beliefs distort our present reality, we become capable of seeing the present moment as it really is. We become like little children again, open and curious about what people are saying and doing without jumping to conclusions, making assumptions, or leaping into defensive or aggressive responses. Then we are able to do what's important for us in that new moment.

HOW TO CHANGE BELIEFS

I want to dramatize just how extraordinary and powerful changing your beliefs can be in helping you to open yourself to new ways of doing what's important for you when things aren't going your way. Imagine that your habits are like a software program on a computer. You like the program, but it's no longer fully meeting your needs. One amazing day, someone comes along and shows you how to modify the "code" that makes your software program run. You carefully punch in the keys that access the hidden code. Hieroglyphic computer-babble appears on your screen. With skill and speed, you modify the code. You press the "Save" button, and bingo! Your computer suddenly knows how to fix itself whenever it breaks down.

Let's take this one step closer to reality. Imagine that you have always felt scared at the sight of a snake. For some unexplained reason, you think that the evil creepy-crawler is intent on sliding up your pant leg and biting your inner thigh. One day, you are walking through the woods when one of the slimy serpents darts out in front of you. This time, however, you feel completely relaxed. You reach down and snatch it up behind its head. What would once have terrified you is now an easy experience.

What has changed? Your beliefs have changed. Everything else has stayed the same. The snake is still long and slimy. But you are no longer feeling a desire to run away from it or to attack it. Instead, you are able to be fully present with it, and to be open and curious about the color of its scaly skin, its bulging dark eyes, and its ever-flickering, forked red tongue. Of course, this is only useful if doing what's right for you in the presence of a snake is what's important now for you.

Imagine how much more useful this would be every time

you face a deep wound like a betrayal from your spouse, the death of a loved one, or living with other people's annoying habits. Suddenly, you could feel safe and centered, even if your world appears to be crashing and burning around you. This is indeed possible, and I have seen people come to peace about scars on their body, about their clean-freak obsession, about being raped, about a permanent handicap, or about their child's illness. I personally came to peace about many beliefs that I had held, including the belief that I needed to have all the right answers, that I would be rejected if I was not a good athlete, that I was a bad person if someone didn't like me, and that something awful might happen to me if I showed my true feelings. The power of changing one's beliefs is extraordinary.

I want to share with you four ways in which you can change your beliefs so that your past experiences do not define your present possibilities. Equally important, there is one way in which your beliefs cannot be changed. Let's look at the four possible ways first:

1. **Life Experiences.** This is the way in which we acquired our beliefs in the first place. This popular route often involves great pain and hardship, whether it's getting stung by a bee or being dumped by a lover. We acquire new beliefs in order to protect us from getting hurt again. If the pain is deep enough, some of us have to hit a brick wall before we will change those cherished beliefs. The more present we are, the more open-minded we become to adapting our old beliefs to fit our present reality, just as a curious two-year-old does.

2. **Self-exploratory Dialogues.** This is when we attempt to question our way to the unconscious beliefs we have, either alone or with a skilled partner. Once conscious, we

can make an intentional choice to change that belief to a new one that better suits how we want to live *now*, rather than remaining stuck with what we learned in the past. This is the method that I used most frequently when I first started working on changing my beliefs.

3. **Reframing.** This is where we consciously choose to look at a situation from a different perspective. For example, instead of feeling annoyed that you are late, you can decide to feel grateful that you even reached your destination in the first place. This is a way to take the pressure off yourself, by changing your perspective about a given situation. I use this method the most often now that I am comfortable with the idea that my beliefs are not set in concrete.

4. **Affirmations.** This is done in the style of Norman Vincent Peale, and the idea is to repeat positive belief statements to ourselves over and over for many days in a row. "I am happy with my golf game. I am happy with my golf game." "I am happy if my house is a mess. I am happy if my house is a mess." This works well because we begin to seek experiences that test and eventually confirm that we can trust our new belief. This is the path most often touted in motivational phrases such as, "Whether you think you can, or whether you think you can't, you are right!"

The one way that does *not* work is for someone to tell us what our belief *should* be. For a variety of reasons, most people's egos will block this out. Just ask any married couple how well it works. "You should clean up the dishes right away!" is one belief. "Who cares if they sit in the sink for a day?" is the partner's response. Each partner is trying to "sell" their beliefs to each other, resulting in the potential for lots of conflict. People feel threatened when they are "pressured" to change. Instead, they tend to resist changing their belief even more resolutely.

The most controllable way to change your beliefs is the second method, **self-exploratory dialogues**. This technique often brings quick results and brings about an immediate and powerful change in how you look at major struggles in your life. Though it is quite simple to explain, it is not so easy to do. You are essentially asking yourself three questions in the form of a reflective, "Socratic" dialogue, as Socrates did in ancient Greece.

1. What is happening?
2. How do you feel about it?
3. Why do you feel that way?

The last question typically uncovers your beliefs about the situation that you are upset about. You will need at least an hour's time to ask yourself these three questions, or variations of them, over and over again. Once you get the hang of it, it is quite fun. Doing a dialogue is like going on an adventure into unexplored territory, uncovering how your own mind works. Beliefs work in layers, and as soon as you uncover one, you will discover one more underneath it. There is an ancient Chinese saying that captures this truism rather well: *"Ask why seven times and you shall know the truth."*

I want to give you an example of how a simple self-exploratory dialogue is done. Let's say a man is working on an important report for work. Suddenly, his software stops working. After doing his best to fix the problem on his own, he pulls out his computer manual and tries to learn more about how to fix it. For some reason, he notices that he numbs out in those moments, meaning that he is not very present. His mind is so filled with the thought that the software "should" be working, that he becomes overwhelmed with frustration. Buried in emotion, he is unable to effectively absorb what he is reading. He is experiencing "temporary frost," limiting his ability to do what is important for him in that moment. He gives up in frustration and calls the software company for help, at the cost of a significant amount of time and money.

Instead, he might choose to do a dialogue to get at the root of his frustration and become more present in order to feel centered about the whole situation. Perhaps he will even come up with a better solution. Here is what a hypothetical dialogue might sound like, as if done between two people (notice that the questioner only asks non-judgmental, non-leading questions):

"What is happening?" *"My #@!&² software is not working!"*

"How do you feel about that?" *"What do you think?"*

The questioner never gets drawn in by answering the explorer's questions: "It doesn't really matter what I think. What matters is what you think and feel." *"Okay, I feel angry."*

"Why do you feel angry?" *"Because this program is supposed to be a good one, and it turns out to be a piece of crap!"*

"This might sound like a dumb question, but why do you believe that the software should be a good one?" *"Because I paid good money for it and besides, three people at work recommended the darn thing."*

"Why does that mean it should be a good one?" *"Because it's supposed to be from a good company, and the product came highly recommended. Instead, it's a piece of junk!"* He pauses... *"Now my report is going to be late."*

"How do you feel about that?" *"Ticked off."*

"Why are you ticked off about that?" *"My boss will be angry with me, and I'll have to work all night to get it done."*

"What is it about that that bothers you?" *"I wanted to spend the night with my wife and kids, not working on this report!"*

"Why do you feel unhappy about that?" *"Well, I promised my wife we'd go out as a family. She's going to be really angry with me when she finds out I have to work."*

"How do you feel about her getting angry with you?" *"Well, who needs the grief? Besides, I wanted to go out, too."*

"What are you afraid might happen if you were not unhappy about this situation?" *"Well, my wife wouldn't be too impressed if I just strolled in and happily told her I've got to work. However, I can see that getting angry about it isn't fixing my software problem. I suppose I could just take the hit from my boss and go out with my family anyway. Maybe he'll understand why I'm late. If he doesn't, well, maybe I could live with that anyway."* He pauses... *"I think I'll call him right now."*

In this short, simple example, this man's belief was that he had to be unhappy in order to deal with his wife's anticipated reaction to his bailing out on her and the kids in order to do his work. By getting clear on it, he could both let go of being angry, and at the same time make a better choice about how to deal with the situation by putting the real problem, his late report, back to his boss instead of in his personal life.

I learned this amazing approach to self-discovery at a place called The Option Institute International Learning & Training Center. The Option Institute was started by a man named Barry Neil Kaufman ("Bears") and his wife Samahria after they achieved an outstanding success in bringing their two-year-old son out of severe autism in the 1970s. Bears wrote a book about this miraculous venture, which NBC later made into a movie called, "Son-Rise" starring James Farentino as Bears.

Bears and Samahria used a refinement of this technique, which they now call The Option Dialogue Process®, to teach the adults working with their young son to be accepting and non-judgmental about his behavior so that they could be fully present with him, even if all he did was spin a plate for two hours straight, while totally ignoring them. This created a tremendously safe environment for their son, allowing him to be the best he could be, as well. Bears and Samahria and their team of volunteers worked with their young son like this for twelve hours a day, seven days a week. After three months, they got just five seconds of eye contact. Yet they persevered, and after nearly two years, their son emerged completely out of his autism. The secret to their success was their ability to stay fully present with their son. Doing self-exploratory dialogues was their method of changing their beliefs so that they could accept his non-response, even after several weeks of intensive efforts that yielded no noticeable results.

You must become conscious of your beliefs if you are to live fully in the present. You will find that you will then make better decisions and wiser choices that not only satisfy others, but most importantly, satisfy you! If you want to learn this technique in much greater depth, I highly recommend Barry Neil Kaufman's book, *To Love Is to Be Happy With*. The author provides many good examples of word-for-word dialogues that demonstrate how other people have come to peace about a variety of distressing issues, from marriage and work to parenting and sexuality. You can find out how to order this book by visiting **www.option.org**, or by contacting your favorite bookseller.

Reframing your beliefs is another simple yet powerful way to feel better about situations that are not in your control. I had an amazing experience with a man who reframed his beliefs about a major event in his life. We were asked to think about one of the worst experiences we had ever had in our lives. Then we were asked to share that story with a fellow participant. The instructor asked us to first tell this story to our partner in as purely factual a way as possible. My partner was Harry,[1] a forty-five-year old successful financier. This is what Harry told me: "My brother died tragically several years ago. His wife was an alcoholic and suffered severe mental health problems. Because of this situation, I agreed to parent their six-year-old son, my nephew. I raised him as if he were my own son. At the age of twenty, he dropped out of university. He is now twenty-five, has no job and no money and is living on the street." Well, that was quite a story, I thought.

The instructor then asked us to tell the story as negatively as possible, as if it were the worst thing that had ever happened to us. Suddenly, the whole room was buzzing as the emotions around the stories came to life. This is what Harry told me: "My brother was killed, and it devastated our family. What made it particularly hard was that his wife, my sister-in-law, was clearly not competent to parent their six-year-old son. She was an alcoholic, depressed, and just plain wacko. My parents came to me and pleaded with me to step in and take care of the boy. It was the *last* thing I wanted to do. I was a young hotshot trader, living a life of booze, women, and partying. But I reluctantly decided to do it anyway. To my surprise, I really got into it. I raised the kid as if he were my own son! I gave him the best of everything— private school, Ivy League university, the whole bit. So what does he do? When he's twenty, he drops out of school. Now he's twenty-five and a bum. He lives on the street. He's good for nothing. He's never had a job, and he won't listen to a thing I say to him. In fact, I haven't spoken to him in two years! I gave him everything and what thanks do I get?"

---

[1]Not his real name

Wow. This time, I really felt the intensity of Harry's story. He was hurt and angry, and I could certainly understand why.

Then our instructor told us to describe the story as if it were the best thing that ever happened to us. The room fell deathly silent. Nobody knew where to begin. Finally, Harry started talking to me: "My brother was killed, and I had the good fortune to take over the parenting responsibility for his six-year-old son. He brought a lot of joy into my life, as I never had children of my own. I spoiled him, I gave him all that I could, and he was a good kid during his entire child-hood. When he grew up, he stopped going to school and decided not to work. (This is where Harry really started to get into it—he was smiling and chuckling more and more as he told this version of his story.) Today he chooses to "live lightly on this earth." He's happy, so why should I begrudge him that?"

I'll never forget that one line: "He chooses to live lightly on this earth." One minute his stepson was a street-bum. The next minute, he was using up as few of the earth's resources as he could, while living his life the way he wanted to. In less than five minutes, Harry had reframed his beliefs about a sit-uation that had caused him a great deal of angst.

Whether his change of perspective was permanent or temporary, I'll never know. My experience with reframing my beliefs is that it does not matter. All that matters is that for the present moment, I am giving myself the experience that I want to have, not the one that my past beliefs are cre-ating for me. This opens the door for me to do what's impor-tant for me in that moment in time. When I am golfing, for example, I sometimes screw up and take seven shots to get on the green, whereas two or three would normally be enough. I walk onto the green feeling frustrated as I look at the long, thirty-foot putt I have to make in two shots in order to avoid scoring a pitiful ten. I feel tense, and I know that this will aggravate my ability to properly judge how hard to hit the ball. In that moment, I reframe my situation. I decide to believe that I am on the green in *two* shots, not seven shots. I visualize past situations where this was the case. Suddenly, I feel my whole body begin to relax as I remember how good I felt. I begin to feel more present. I let go of my seven poor shots—shots that are now in the past and out of my control. Invariably, I end up making a fine putt. Even if I don't, I *feel* better in the moment.

One of the instructors at Option once told us that she had slowly discovered that everything we see, hear, and think is based on a belief. She said, "It is one giant 'make-beliefs" world out there." I agree with her. And if it is all "make-belief," why not make up beliefs that help you be the best you can be in the moment, regardless of what other people believe, or what you believed to be true in the past?

A WARNING

I must tell you about one thing that you may face which happened to me when I began to explore my beliefs: You may become difficult to live with for awhile. There is something about becoming conscious of your beliefs that affects people whom I know that have gone down this path, including myself: They tend to become quite judgmental of others.

For example, my wife Pam (now my ex-wife) and I realized after our first weekend together at Option that we had both acquired many habits that were filled with beliefs and judgments. These habits would easily "trigger" us. We were in a rut of "knowing" that certain past phrases or actions would predictably lead to something we did not like or want, leaving us instantly feeling angry and annoyed with each other. "Honey, I want to go shopping..." Wham! That phrase would hit me, and I would react in a heartbeat. "Shopping? Is that *all* you ever want to do?" It was hard for me to wait for her to finish her sentence when I was so sure I knew what it was that she was going to say. If I had been present, I would not have made those assumptions. I would have waited for her to tell me the whole story, and then responded to her.

Once I became aware of her beliefs about shopping, my reaction became more intense. I felt even *more* resentful about her shopping. Previously, I tolerated this and many other habits of hers mostly because I was unable to pinpoint why I felt so irritated about them. Now that I could "see" her beliefs, I was able to attack them more directly. "How can anyone believe that going shopping makes you feel good about yourself? It's just an exhausting waste of time and energy!" What I was doing was judging her beliefs. I was trying to shame her into buying my belief and giving up hers. Of course, I did that unconsciously for reasons that I later learned were *why* I was so poor at being present with her or anyone.

The good news about exploring my beliefs was that I felt like I was opening my eyes for the first time. I became aware that I had allowed other people's belief systems to "make" me feel guilty for much of my life. With my new awareness of beliefs, I began to recognize when others were trying to "sell" me their beliefs, right in the moment. This let me become more effective at resisting feeling pressured into doing things that I did not want to do.

However, as I became skilled at rebuffing them, I fell into the trap of trying to convince them that their feelings and hurts were based on their beliefs and that "they should just change their beliefs, and then they would feel better." Even worse, I began trying to get others to change their belief system to match mine! After all, I became very good at identifying and explaining what beliefs were, whereas for most people, beliefs remained a cloudy, misty subject resting deeply in their unconscious! Mere mortals had no chance against me and my knowledge of beliefs! However, you can be sure that mere mortals are not stupid. They unconsciously recognized that I was trying to change their beliefs. They began to either avoid me, or to dig in and resist me, including becoming quite angry with me. Despite these risks, I encourage you to dive in. Becoming aware of and capable of changing your beliefs is a necessary skill if you want to discover what's important for you in this present moment.

Here are some closing thoughts about *Change Your Beliefs*...

Remember...
- Your beliefs color everything you see, hear, and experience. Knowing what your beliefs are allows you to adapt flexibly and wisely to whatever is actually happening.
- Your beliefs serve you by helping you judge what is safe or unsafe for you and for others. They are the "rules of life" that trigger your emotions and guide you to what was once the right thing for you, based on your past experiences.
- You will tend to automatically seek information that confirms your beliefs, while rationalizing and rejecting information that conflicts with your beliefs. This leaves your mind partially closed, limiting your ability to see and hear what is actually happening.
- "It's not about you." You cannot "make" someone feel something, though your behavior may be the spark that triggers their emotional reaction. They are reacting to their beliefs, just as you are reacting to your own set of beliefs.

Watch for...
- The discomfort that comes when you first try on a new belief. Like folding your arms in a way that you've never

folded them before, it will feel uncomfortable and fake. Trust yourself that this feeling will go away.

- The temptation of wanting to convert other people to your beliefs, or using your knowledge of beliefs to manipulate others. This is a seductive trap.

Try this...
- Focus on a "magical" time in your life when you felt like a "winner." What were you believing about yourself? What is stopping you from believing those same things today?
- Reframe your beliefs in the moment. Visualize how you would *prefer* to perceive your predicament and see if you relax, feel better, and make wiser decisions.
- Do a self-exploratory dialogue with a trusted friend, who agrees to only ask questions and never offer advice during the dialogue, even if you ask for it.

At this stage of your journey, you will have some new and positive experiences in which you trusted yourself enough to take down some walls and to feel the joy that comes from letting go of old and debilitating beliefs that were burdening you. You will taste the joy that comes from feeling free to decide what's right for you, rather than letting your unconscious beliefs rule your life. However, you will find that you cannot change all your beliefs, nor do you even *want* to change certain beliefs in order to feel safe and present. At some point in time, you will find that you cannot melt seamlessly into the world around you. Instead, you must dare to let yourself and the world see what you really think and feel in the present moment.

Be Authentic

THE DANGER ZONE

You discover who you really are when you are living fully in the present. You say and do what you really think and feel. You don't filter it, hide it, or otherwise disguise it. In these moments, everything about you is genuine. Your words line up with your actions. Your body language lines up with your feelings. You dare to say and do things that you always wanted to, but were too afraid to risk. You speak up when you used to shut up. You stand tall when you used to walk out small. You laugh and cry when you used to withdraw and stifle. You expose your deepest feelings, your darkest secrets, and your most blissful whimsies without fear, if it is useful to do so. When you are this way, you are being authentic.

When you are authentic without an intent to harm others, you give yourself an awesome feeling, which is the feeling of self-love. You are choosing to be who you really are, rather than a version of you that is more perfect and more acceptable to those around you. You have no need to be *better* than the real you anymore. In these moments, you are accepting that you are good enough as you are, paradoxically allowing yourself to do what's important for you in that moment, even if that isn't as good as you or someone else would have liked in retrospect.

Most of us fall short of this ideal state. I certainly did, and I still do. But I remain committed to being as authentic as I can be anyway. Being authentic is the only way in which you can discover what's right for the person you really are, hidden behind your protective walls. When you speak and act based on what you really think and feel, you can no longer hide. You can no longer deny the good, the bad, and the ugly parts of who you are. Then you become capable of knowing yourself well enough to truly *know* what's important now for you.

Being authentic can be dangerous. You risk offending people who matter to you when you tell them what you really think and how you really feel. The Jim Carey movie, *Liar Liar*, parodies this danger to great comedic effect. By the power of a spell cast upon him by his five-year-old son's birthday wish, Jim Carey's character becomes incapable of telling a lie. He sees a woman with large breasts in the elevator, and tells her exactly what he is lustfully thinking. As a lawyer, he tells the judge precisely what lies he is telling in order to get his guilty client off the hook. Everyone around him starts to become very angry with him. He is being authentic, and he is paying a price for it.

Yet, there is a price to be paid for *not* being authentic. We pay a price every time we bend the truth, hold back how we feel, and conform to what others want from us. We build up a storehouse of wounds and resentments linked to the people from whom we have held back our truth. This storehouse of wounds is our past. When a new wound comes along, we remember our storehouse. These memories fuel our anger and fear in this present moment. We must purge ourselves of this storehouse of resentments if we want to live in the present. How to do this "purging" without having an intent to harm those around us is the foundation to learning how to live in the present lovingly and authentically.

When you are authentic, you open yourself to discovering what you unconsciously *believe* is what's important for you, even if it's not necessarily "good for you." Being authentic uncovers the dreams that you may privately have, yet are afraid to admit. Maybe you have had your heart set on achieving a certain career position, on having children, on finding a soul mate, or on fulfilling certain sexual desires. When you repress these dreams that linger within you, they are the future hanging over you and telling you that your past has not given you what you wanted. These dreams cloud your ability to live in the present. Claiming them by being authentic about them is how you will rise above them, by either pursuing them or by letting them die as mere fantasies that you don't really want after all.

Being authentic is an *in-the-moment* struggle in which you feel torn: A waiter is giving you slow service, and you feel an urge to tell him to get moving! A driver cuts you off, and you want to lash out in anger. Someone is unexpectedly kind to you, and you feel like crying or hugging them, but you hold back. Your spouse is pressuring you to do something you don't want to do, but you go along with it anyway. Someone flirts with you seductively, and you know that going down that path isn't right for you, but you do it anyway. These are but a few of the many moments each day when each of us encounters the doorway called *Be Authentic*.

In these moments, we are faced with a dilemma: Do I choose me?...or, do I choose the other person? Many times, we will choose the other person. We have deep-seated beliefs that we shouldn't hurt their feelings. While I don't dispute the wisdom of being kind to others, being authentic means being conscious of whether you really *want* to be kind, or whether you are putting on a false mask so that they will *think* you are kind.

Personally, I discovered that as I looked at my beliefs more deeply, I had a belief that was underneath all of my other beliefs. I believed that *I needed the approval of others.* This belief motivated me to choose in favor of the other person so that I wouldn't hurt their feelings, or so that they would be impressed with me in some way. I did this at the expense of what was truly important for me in key areas of my life that often left me feeling bad about myself. When we continuously choose the other person for protective reasons, we are actually abandoning ourselves. This self-abandonment is a major cause of resentment and anger. In those moments, we are not doing what's important now for some part of who we are. Instead, we are overriding that part of us so that we say and do what we "believe" will be acceptable to others. Each time we do this, we are suppressing a part of ourselves out of fear that we will regret speaking our authentic truth.

The danger you face is that the pent-up anger from years of suppressing yourself will emerge in an explosive and harmful way. As I became more committed to not abandoning myself in this way, I found it harder and harder to suppress how I really felt. One day, for example, I was driving in downtown Toronto, when the traffic lights turned yellow. Two cars went through the yellow light, but the third one in front of me wisely chose to stop just as the light turned red.

I, on the other hand, had every intention of going through that light myself because I was late for an appointment. When that driver stopped, I felt a powerful rage sweep over me and a nearly uncontrollable desire to ram his car right into the intersection and to go through regardless! Somehow I controlled myself enough to stop. As I did, I shook my open hand at the driver in front of me in anger, even as I felt some fear at my open display of anger and emotion. I didn't have the guts to give him the middle finger, which was what I really wanted to do. To my shock, the driver actually opened his door, looked back at me and calmly said in a loud voice, "The light turned red." My anger instantly disappeared. I smiled sheepishly at him and hollered back, "You're right."

I would never have expressed such anger nor felt so tempted to do something so incredibly reckless when all my walls were safely suppressing my true emotions. Yet, this emotional reaction was my authentic self! A nasty part of my real self came right out in public for the whole world to see! The lesson I kept learning over and over was that being authentic is DANGEROUS! That guy might have gotten out of his car with a baseball bat in his hand!

This is the risk of choosing to be who you really are in the present moment. If you are fully present, then you will be authentic. If you are authentic, you may say or do something that might "make" someone angry. If someone becomes angry with you, you might feel bad. They, in turn, might even hurt you. Then you might react to their anger and do something harmful that you may really regret! This is how full-scale battles often begin.

Overcoming your fear that you will do something that you might later regret is crucial to learning how to live your life in the present. You must face the fear that some part of you may be mean, shallow, or selfish. The paradox in this

journey is that in order to overcome and ultimately eliminate these "bad" qualities in you, you must risk exposing
them. You have to risk the possibility that yes, indeed, part
of you is mean, selfish, hurtful, and even violent. By being
authentic, you allow yourself to see these parts of the real
you, to accept them and then to trust that you can control
them enough to be safely authentic.

In the men's group with Dr. André Stein that I attended
for two-and-a-half years, we often complained about how
our spouses accused us of various crimes like "always being
selfish and insensitive." André would come back at us and
say, "And is it ever true?"

"Well, sure, sometimes it is true," one of us would
answer back.

"Okay," he would then say, "Tell her that. Own it. 'Sometimes it is true that I am selfish and insensitive. And often I
am not!" he added with a flourish.

By owning these qualities in ourselves, we become capable of eliminating them. Our fear is that if we accept that we
are selfish and insensitive, we are giving ourselves permission to be that way even more! Yet, I found the opposite was
what actually happened. Once I accepted these qualities, I
became capable of staying fully present in situations in
which the real me might have previously lashed out or run
away, thereby escaping the present and not doing what was
important for me in that moment.

If you are afraid that you might blow up with anger at
your meddling mother, your critical boss, or your insensitive
spouse, you will probably avoid being authentic with them.
In fact, you will probably want to avoid them as much as
possible, period! Yet by avoiding them, you are suppressing
part of who you are, thereby limiting your own happiness
and peace of mind. Unless you can change your beliefs

about these people and their annoying habits, the only way for you to discover what's important for you in similar situations is to be authentic with them. Then you will see who you really are and what you believe is right for you in this present moment.

Let's say you are waiting third in line at the bank and someone steps right in front of everyone, going directly to a teller the moment she becomes available. What do you do? Perhaps you hope the teller will send the person away. Let's say she doesn't. Then what do you do? Perhaps you hope the person at the front of the line will speak up, objecting to this rude intrusion. But what if both people in front of you say nothing? What would you do? If you say nothing, will you be at peace with that, or will you want to give that person a dirty look when they turn away to leave? If you say something, what would you say? "Excuse me, sir, there is a lineup here, and you are welcome to join it right behind me." That seems reasonably polite. Perhaps the authentic you is a little more indignant than that. You walk right up to the person, tap them on the shoulder, and say, "Hey! Just who the hell do you *think* you are? The rest of us back here have been waiting in line for *ten* minutes! Do you *mind* getting in line and not butting in?" Whew. That's tough talk! What if the intruder turns around and says, "I have been here for half an hour already. I am merely completing a transaction that I began before you arrived. Please mind your own business!" Ooh! How embarrassing!

When you are authentic, you see who you really are. You see how you handle the unexpected reactions of others to your authenticity. You discover what you currently believe is the right thing to do for you, in this particular situation. Since living in the present is always based on the situation you are presently in, doing this hundreds of times over months and years is how you form a clear picture of the real you. Every time you are authentic in a pressure-filled situation, you give yourself the opportunity to acquire new beliefs about what's important now for you, regardless of how you've done things in the past.

No matter how much logic I give you on being authentic, you will likely find that at the moment of truth, you will still feel yourself quivering in your boots. Personally, I could always see that huge door with the big "FEAR" word on it. I feared that even if I got away with being authentic, I would hear the voices of my friends speaking behind my back, saying, "Oh, he used to be such a nice guy. I don't know what's happened to him!" as they resolved to avoid me thereafter.

When you are authentic, you are wide open to being judged. People may criticize you, hurt you, gossip about you, and humiliate you if you say and do things with which they disagree. Therein lies the fear of being authentic. Someone might not like what you really think or feel. Someone might get angry with you, and then you'll have to deal with that. The more that you fear how someone will react to your truth, the more likely you are to avoid being authentic and to concede to their wishes.

Unfortunately, this inner truth of yours does not go away just because you decided to avoid the possibility of conflict. While the other person may not know that you swallowed hard, some inner part of *you* knows that you did. You will know this to be true if you experience feelings of resentment and hostility afterwards. This is the point at which your inauthentic behavior lays down a "past" with that person that will interfere with your ability to live in the present. This past event requires a wall behind which to contain it. The wall acts like a dam, keeping your own anger within, while protecting you from letting that person stick it to you again. An old boss of mine used to say, "Screw me once ... your fault. Screw me twice ... my fault." Walls protect us from getting screwed again.

We build walls when we decide that this person could hurt us. In truth, you have also become dangerous. With enough unresolved hurts and wounds, your wall is all that stands between the real you and your pent-up hurt feelings. Sooner or later, the proverbial straw may land that will break the camel's back, bringing all those past wounds and resentments back to the present. If that happens, look out! Of course, that day may never arrive. You may suppress your resentments so effectively that you never boil over. Then your only danger is that they will boil within you, invading your health and well-being, as described in **Listen to Your Body**.

There is always a price to pay. Many of us find a "safe" alternative outlet for venting our pent-up frustrations. If we have a bad day at the office where work went off the rails, bosses were unhappy, and traffic was snarled, we may come home and kick the dog for jumping on us out of joy. We get moody with our spouse and short-tempered with our kids, even though they really didn't do anything to deserve our wrath. We rage at other drivers, far beyond what their "crime" actually deserved.

These mostly innocent bystanders are paying the price for our unwillingness to be authentic with the person towards whom we are really angry. This is not a prize that most of our friends and family are eagerly seeking out. Yet, because we know that they will not fire us or abandon us (at least not today), we let our authentic anger emerge. While this may go a long way towards letting our steam boil off, it does nothing to endear us to those whom we love! Sooner or later, they are going to have a major problem with us.

Unless they are authentic with us at the time of our blasting, they, too, will begin to build up resentments towards us. Not being authentic results in hot lava spilling onto the wrong people, or spilling within one's inner being. The price tag of being inauthentic is high. Our own emotional health and that of those around us depend on our ability to speak our truth. Yet, speaking up authentically remains a frightening and dangerous prospect for most of us.

The prize we receive when we remove our walls is that we give ourselves a chance to reclaim who we really are. This is that part of us that is the best that we can be. This is the person that we experienced when we were soaring, at peace with the world, and accepting of ourselves. You can recognize this feeling from a time when you fell in love. What is romantic love but the glorious feeling that one person, one special, crazy, insane person accepts you as you are, warts, and all? Imagine if that special person who accepted all of you, were *you?* Then you could feel loved all the time. When I feel loved, I feel capable of being fully present as the best person I can be, imperfect as that may be. Being authentic is the doorway to discovering the self-acceptance that you are good enough and no longer need to hide who you really are. Then you will truly become capable of knowing and doing what's important for you.

THREE TYPES OF THINKING

In order to live more fully in the present, we must become aware of what is actually going on inside our mind. As you become more aware of the beliefs you have that are triggering you in day-to-day situations, from how the dishes get done to how your spouse treats you, you will begin to notice the thoughts that are actually happening inside your head. This is when you are starting to live more consciously, which is the essence of living in the present. At this stage of your journey, your main challenge is to *notice* what's happening inside your mind. The thoughts you are having will tell you what's important now for you, whether you like those thoughts or not.

For many of us, what's important now is to *think*. Thinking is an extremely effective way to escape being present. Instead of being connected to the world around us, we are living inside our heads. This serves us by giving us a sense of control. The less we feel in control, the more we find that thinking is an attractive way to get back the feeling of being in control. As I slowed down my mind (by slowing down my life), I began to see what those thoughts actually were.

We are thinking in one of three ways. We are thinking about the future, trying to figure out how to make life unfold the way we want it to. We are thinking about the past, trying to rationalize that what we said or did was really okay. Or, we are fantasizing about what we wish were happening in the present moment, rather than what is really happening. These are the three ways in which we try to *mentally* alter our present reality. We are trying to take control of what's happening in our lives, rather than merely accepting and adapting to it. This is quite understandable, yet all these thoughts are what block you from being fully present. When half your brain is busily thinking, then your ability to see, hear, listen, and understand other people is dramatically reduced. Personally, I was able to reverse my poor memory merely by learning how to stop all that noise inside my own head. If you can understand why thinking about the past or the future is often what's important now for you, you give yourself the opportunity to let it go. Then you will feel free to live more fully in the present, trusting that what's past is past, and what is yet to come is not yet in your hands to worry about. You will then feel much clearer about what's right for you to do in this present moment.

Let's look more closely at these three types of thinking:

1. **Role-play-thinking** is where we role-play future conversations with others and thereby try to predict what they might say or do. Our purpose is to overcome any possible objections or accusations that might come our way. We want to be sure that what we're about to do will be acceptable *and* successful. We may also be having future conversations that justify our past behavior with the aim of getting another person to understand and accept our version of what happened.

2. **Replay-thinking** is where we re-enact past conversations and events, searching to affirm that what we did was acceptable, or to beat ourselves up for making a mistake. We want to justify that any offences we committed were innocent accidents, or someone else's fault. In addition, we are looking for flaws in our original role-play thinking, so that we will know how to be "better" next time, and to find ways to "correct" any mistakes we might have made.

3. **Fantasy-thinking** generally allows us to revel in how brilliant or popular we were or will be. This is when we invent solutions, imagine what a finished project will look like, or self-indulge about how terrific we'll feel if or when success comes our way. Fantasy-thinking is attractive because we always say and do the right thing, and others marvel at how terrific we are.

Role-play-thinking helps us to not make mistakes. Personally, I wanted to have every angle thought out. I wanted to take no chances that something could go wrong, or that I had missed some important aspect of a decision. I did not want to suffer the embarrassment or humiliation of making a mistake. In that way, I was a perfectionist. Perfectionism is a huge obstacle to living in the present. We have to learn how to accept our imperfection and embrace our mistakes if we are ever going to be fully present. My fear was that I might not be perceived as smart enough if I had not pre-thought out every possibility to justify what I was doing or how I was planning to do it.

I did a lot of role-play-thinking about work projects. If the project was a business report, I would sometimes wake up first thing in the morning and draft the entire report in my head while tossing and turning in my bed. Why couldn't I trust myself that the right words would come out when I actually sat down at my computer? Why did I need to play it out in my head first? I also struggled with this on projects around the house. I pictured each step of the project in my mind in explicit detail, like what wood I would need, where I would put it, how I would cut it, sand it, paint it, and finish it. I could do the same once it was over, reveling in how wonderfully the project turned out. Of course, these were all moments spent in my head, and not in the present. Even while I was on vacation, I often did role-play-thinking, imagining just how thrilled others would be when I told them what wonderful experiences I had had. I was actually living in the future in those moments, rather than fully enjoying the sights and sounds of that moment of my vacation.

Role-play-thinking also happens when we are anticipating an argument with someone. If my wife wanted us to go away for the weekend and I did not, I could *not* simply say that. That was not good enough. I had to have a better reason than that! So I would play out the entire conversation in my head, looking for a way to explain why staying at home was a better idea. First, I would try out an opening: "Well, I know dear, that you've worked hard and want a rest, but I don't feel like driving that far up north." This would be my trial balloon, my opening. Then I would imagine her response. "You didn't mind driving up there last month when you had two golf games lined up with the guys!" I could just hear the indignation in her voice. Then I would search for a comeback answer.

"Well, that was different. I...I...I..." Then I would give up on that one. It just didn't fly. So I would try a different one.

"Dear, you know that trip up north that you want to take, well, I don't think we can afford it this month." A-ha! That felt better.

Again, I would imagine her response. "Of course, we can afford it. We have $5000 worth of credit left on our gold card."

"Yeah but," I would respond in my mind, "I don't want any more debt." Now I've got her, I would think to myself.

Then she would respond in my mind, "Well, my bonus is looking good, and I'm sure we'll be able to pay it off at the end of the year. I really want this trip. I have worked so hard. I need a break!" I could feel myself losing the battle. Of course, there really wasn't a battle. At least, not with her. This was all going on inside my own head. Not that I was as stupid as I may sound! I was relying on our history to make some educated assumptions about what I could expect her response to be.

If I decided to give it up based on the role-play-thinking I did in my head, I would just say, "Fine, let's go up north." In her mind, it was all very easy. She made the suggestion to go up north, and I agreed. In my mind, it wasn't that simple at all. I felt some resentment at her "victory," one that she did not even realize she had won and I had lost. By not being authentic, I was deciding that what I wanted was not important enough. Avoiding conflict was what was important now for me in that moment, at the expense of being true to myself.

Years later, I was giving a speech on the topic of present living when a woman came up to me afterwards and said that she could strongly identify with this "role-play-thinking." She told me that just the previous week, she was having breakfast with her husband. He was reading the paper while she was eating...and thinking. Suddenly, she looked up at him and said, "Okay." He looked at her strangely and said, "Okay what? What are you talking about?" She realized in that moment that she had had an entire conversation in her head with him on whether or not to they should sell their house, something he had been trying to get her to agree to for some time. The conversation was so real for her that she did not even realize for a moment that he was not a participant! When she admitted this to him, he responded, "You are scaring me! I think you better get some help!" Coincidentally, she stumbled upon my speaking seminar a week later...

A major problem with role-play-thinking is that we are not able to be present with the person or situation when it actually happens. In the above example, my wife simply had to say the words, "Of course, we can afford it..." and my mind would just fill in the rest of the conversation, leaving me angry at her before she had even really given her reasons! She did not have to give them. I already knew them from my role-play-thinking, right? Wrong! I just *assumed* I knew what she would say. Oh, how those assumptions blocked my ability to have a real conversation in the present! My role-play-thinking got completely in my way.

Now let's look at **Replay-thinking**. This is popular for those of us who love to live in the past where replay-thinking is anchored. Replay-thinking happens when we turn on our mental VCR and play back an actual conversation or event, confirming that what we did was good enough. When the replay is about something positive, well, it wasn't just good enough, it was sometimes fantastic! When I finished an achievement of some kind, I often spent a lot of time replaying how wonderfully well I did it, and how impressed others ought to be with my efforts. Replay-thinking was a way to feed my ego, and to affirm that what I had said or done deserved to be approved of and even praised by others. Authentically sharing this thinking with others is sometimes called "bragging."

Another source of re-play-thinking is when we make a mistake. I could spend a great deal of time and energy coming up with different reasons and scenarios to explain why I was late, forgot the milk, didn't have my report done on time, couldn't come to my parents' house for a visit, or said the "wrong" thing. This is sometimes known as rationalizing. My therapist, André, once said to me, "The definition of rationalizing is *bad logic*." Re-play-thinking was a way for me to hide my mistakes, or to convince myself that I was fine and that the problem was the other person or an unfair circumstance. I would run trial conversations in my head with the person to whom I felt I would have to explain myself, trying on different justifications and role-playing with what I might expect the other person to say to me. If I couldn't successfully rationalize my mistake, then I was left feeling bad about myself. Avoiding feeling bad about ourselves is a major incentive to make replay thinking what's important now, rather than facing what really did happen, and what we really did do, regardless of the reasons and circumstances. When we are present, we own our words and actions, no matter what.

A major problem with replay thinking is that, unlike a real VCR, our memory is not perfect. In the heat of the moment, we are often not fully present, which leaves our mind unable to remember what was really said. Instead, we are remembering the pain of the emotions that we felt. We are therefore at risk that our replay thinking will be inaccurate, leading us to aggravate our situation as we withdraw or attack the other person, or even beat up ourselves for the "bad" thing that happened.

Finally, let's look at **Fantasy-thinking**. This is popular for those of us who feel easily bored. Fantasizing is a way to make the present moment far more interesting than it appears to be as we wait in traffic, procrastinate in our work, or sit around at a family function. I could take a challenge from work and chew on it for hours. As a business strategist for most of my career, looking at alternatives and weighing the pros and cons of various ways of achieving a goal was the very nature of my work. The bigger the business, the more choices I had, and the more I could spend time churning over ideas, looking for ways to be brilliant. That was a major motive for me, although I didn't want to admit it to myself until I began to actually *notice* my thoughts. At the time, I believed I was just trying to do a good job. While that was partially true, deep down, I was looking for ways to impress my boss or my client with how smart I was. Coming up with clever ideas was one of my favorite ways of getting the rewards and recognition that I wanted…the approval that I was seeking.

The major problem with fantasy-thinking is that our mind wants to go there instead of being in the here and now. These fantasies, whether they are about career glory, romantic dreams, sexual conquests, or a satisfying revenge, take us instantly out of the present. We will often miss out on what's right for us because part of our mind is occupied with something other than what is actually happening.

In this early part of the journey, you need to *slow* your mind down enough to see what the blur is that makes up your thoughts. When you see what you are actually thinking and feeling in the moment, you can begin to risk openly disclosing those thoughts and feelings. Until you do that, you are in danger of remaining a creature of unconscious habit, driven by your belief system. Like Pavlov's dog that salivated every time the dinner bell rang, you render yourself incapable of adapting to what's important for you in this new present moment.

THREE WAYS TO BE AUTHENTIC

The late Diana, Princess of Wales, whose every move was being watched by the public, was once quoted as saying that she had finally learned that, "What other people think of me is none of my business." With a belief such as that, we can consider the possibility of letting others see our true thoughts, feelings, and desires, without feeling compelled to role-play, replay, or create a fantasy version of who we really are.

In my own case, I anchored my early courage to be more authentic in my belief that other people's feelings are "not about me." If you struggle with being authentic, you need to examine your beliefs for all the reasons why you believe you should "protect" others from their feelings which might emerge from your truth. The opposite of being authentic is to be protective. You need to ask yourself how being protective serves you. What are you afraid would happen if you said and did what you really believe is right for you? Being authentic is the path to self-discovery and self-trust.

Being authentic requires us to commit to truthfulness. When I was rationalizing my past words or deeds, I was searching for reasons and justifications that were bigger, better, and more convincing than just the truth. This left me open to stretching the truth from time to time. My wife became quite conscious of my tendency to quote that well-known expert called "everyone." You know, "*Everyone* I know goes golfing Sunday afternoons. You're the only one who wants me to stay home!" as I tried to manipulate her into agreeing with what I wanted to do.

Another good example of this is the "You never" and "I always" game. "You *never* cooperate when I want to go somewhere, but I *always* do whatever it is that you want to do." I did not see it as lying, though it clearly was. In truth, she often did cooperate. Equally, sometimes I did not do what she wanted. These statements reflected my own feeling of powerlessness. That I wanted to go somewhere different from her was not good enough for me. I had to justify it by exaggerating the truth. Of course, that demonstrated my strong belief that my behavior must be approved of by others, especially by her.

Yet, I could ignore the need for approval when it suited me. This is one of the ironies of "beliefs." Contradictory beliefs can exist right beside each other. I could vehemently use the "everyone" argument in one breath, and just as vehemently say in the next breath, "And if everyone jumped into the lake, would you jump in, too?" As I became more present and conscious of my own habits and language, I was amazed at how often this happened, and with a straight face no less!

Here are three actions that have helped me to find the courage to be truthful and authentic:

1. **"What is the worst thing that can happen, and can I live with it?"** Pause and ask yourself this question right in the moment in which you are wrestling with being authentic. In the few seconds that this takes, you can try to gauge what you might be trying to protect yourself and the other person from, what your authentic choices are, and whether what you are about to say or do will be useful or harmful to others.

2. **Self-disclose first, accuse later.** When I am authentic, I find that if I get a nasty backlash from others, it is often because I made assumptions that turned out to be wrong. Before I make any quick accusations, I try to cool off enough to ask a question that will confirm whether I am out of line, such as, "When you asked me what the heck I was doing, were you trying to suggest that I was doing something wrong?" Assuming you might be misunderstanding the other person and asking open-ended questions to find out, can save you a lot of misery and build trust in yourself that you will be usefully authentic, rather than lashing out at someone in error.

3. **Take action.** When you feel torn about something that really matters to you, doing something beats doing nothing. Doing nothing *guarantees* that you will feel inner turmoil, stress, and anxiety. Taking action may also give you anxiety, but you will have something to work with in terms of understanding what you really wanted and why you were thinking and feeling that way. Some part of you is unhappy with what is happening. Recognize this as valuable information. Taking action will lead you to discovering what your motives *really* are, and what you thought was important for you in that moment, even if it turns out to be less than optimal.

Being authentic in the moment is a difficult choice to make. For many of us, years of training have taught us that people will get angry with us, hold grudges, say bad things about us, or otherwise try to harm us if we speak our truth in difficult situations. I found that I had to open many more doorways to overcome these fears. For now, what matters is that you become aware and accepting of these kinds of thoughts, irrational or undesirable as some of them might be.

THE BEST CONFIDENCE BUILDER

Being authentic is the greatest confidence builder that I have ever experienced. When I was sixteen, I was a shy kid who was barely able to shave. My self-esteem was quite low. I remember wishing as hard as I could that somehow I could just have the confidence that other kids seemed to have. I wished there was a magic potion I could use and just say "Abracadabra!" and poof, I would be the most self-confident person in high school. But it never happened—until years later when I discovered being authentic. When you are authentic, you are choosing *you*. When you are choosing you, you are giving yourself a huge boost of confidence. You are saying to yourself, "Self, you are worth it. Your wants and feelings matter, even if the other person doesn't like what they are." Wow, what a feeling!

When you hide from others what you are really thinking and feeling, you are also hiding yourself from your thoughts and feelings. When you expose your truth to them, you can see them and claim them. Only when you claim them can you really *change* them so that you can make wiser choices in the moment, rather than letting your past habits define your present experience. A friend of mine who re-introduced me to Christianity loved to quote the Bible, where it says, "The truth will set you free."[2] While he had a different intention in mind, speaking your truth is the doorway by which you can set yourself free. Free to be the real you. You no longer have any reason to feel afraid of what someone might think about you if they discovered the "truth" about what you really think or feel. When you are consistently authentic, they already know! When you trust yourself enough to be authentic to this degree, you give yourself the

---

[2]John 8:32,NIV

confidence to stand up and do what's important now for you in any situation.

I found it helpful to understand why we do *not* want to be authentic. The main reason for many of us is that we are trying to control what other people think of us. This is anchored in our need for the approval of others. Burdened by that need, you will have to do what I did—weigh out your thoughts with care, or not say anything at all. This is hard work because you have to constantly stop and filter your real self. We pay a heavy price physically when we swallow our truth, as I mentioned in the first chapter of this book, **Listen to Your Body**. We also risk feeling drained emotionally, mentally, and spiritually. We are fighting against ourselves, resisting our natural desire to be honest in order to present a version of ourselves that we believe will be acceptable to others.

In theory, you can get around this need to be acceptable to others if you always just agree with whatever they want. This is the basis of many "pleaser" types of behavior. Pleasers are trying to find ways to do what is right for themselves while *also* not offending anyone at the same time. They are trying to have their cake and eat it, too. The problem is that this often leads to manipulation and other sorts of deceptive behavior. Many relationships break down because one person is unwilling to be fully authentic about what they want and how they feel. Instead, they begin to find ways to meet their needs behind the back of the other person. This is particularly true emotionally and sexually, as people explore other ways to get the love they want. Once you have broken your commitment to another person without disclosing this breach, whether it's a sabotaged business agreement or sexual infidelity, you have created a past that now hangs over you. You must hide part of who you are, watching what you say and what you do in order to keep your secret.

What you've done in the past is a part of who you are. In order to live fully in the present, you must claim that past, even if you were the innocent victim of another person's selfish and cruel invasion of your rights. We often want to hide these "ugly" parts of what happened to us. For many of us, this unhappy past is anchored in our childhood relationship with our parents. As adults, we begin to see and to appreciate that some of the things our parents did left us with deep scars. They may have beaten us, ignored us, shamed us, or overly controlled every little thing we did. For some people, this unhappy past includes having been sexually molested or raped, having attempted suicide, having done drugs, or some type of "unacceptable" sexual behavior ranging from promiscuity to homosexuality. Hiding these kinds of past wounds requires a wall for each and every one of them. The only way to remove that wall is to claim the wound. When you face that frightening possibility by telling someone about your past, whose approval you fear to lose, you will have truly found the freedom that comes from crossing the doorway of being authentic.

No More Façades

When you are hiding part of who you really are, you are believing that some other people will not find acceptable certain parts of what you think is right for you. Harville Hendrix, in his best-selling book, *Getting the Love You Want*, describes three types of "selfs" that all of us are typically trying to hide. These are:

"1. Your "*lost self*,"—those parts of your being that you had to repress because of the demands of society.
2. Your "*false self*,"—the façade you erected in order to fill the void created by this repression and by a lack of adequate nurturing.

3. Your *"disowned self"*—the negative parts of your false self that met with disapproval and were therefore denied."[3]

This framework of how we hide who we are helped me to accept that I had been inauthentic for very understandable reasons. Our lost self is that part of us from which we have totally disconnected. It is the part that our parents repeatedly told us was "bad," such as when boys learn that "big boys don't cry." For me, my lost self was ultimately the part of me that, deep down, I fervently hoped was lovable, kind, and good enough just as I was. Our false self is that part of us that we have erected that we think will make us acceptable to others, like my image as a successful businessman, or perhaps your image as a super mom, a great athlete, or a good husband. Our disowned self is that part of ourselves that we perceive to be negative, such as our selfishness, our laziness, our pettiness, and so on. To keep these qualities hidden, we must deny them or project them onto others. Hendrix's example is, "What do you mean, I'm lazy? *You're* lazy!"[4]

We hide the ugly parts of ourselves by disowning them, while claiming parts of ourselves that are not real through our false self. Understanding these three types of your "self" will help you to recognize them in the moment and then reclaim them. When you do, you will feel the tremendous joy that comes from accepting another part of the real you, for better or for worse.

Each time you face an aspect of the real you that you have not wanted to see or claim, you will face a deep-seated fear. After all, you constructed these façades for reasons that

---

[3] Getting the Love You Want, Harville Hendrix, 1988, 32

[4] Ibid, 32

served you. Taking them away means exposing the real you that you originally felt was too dangerous to be seen by anyone! You will feel vulnerable in two ways. First, if you act on who you really are, your disowned self might emerge and verbally, if not physically, attack another person. Certainly, my desire to ram the car in front of me into the intersection reflected my instinctive desire to attack someone who was in the way of my getting what I wanted—to arrive on time! Second, if you expose your disowned self, others might use your openness to harm you. For example, I once had a boss who used my angry words about our company management to help escort me out the door within a couple of days. When I was a pre-teen, I often threw temper tantrums, crying or yelling in order to get my way—from arguing about whether the puck was actually in the net to whether I received a fair mark from my teacher. One day, my friends kicked me out of the gang via a nasty letter they had left in my locker. I felt crushed and devastated. I never cried again for twenty-seven years. I was too afraid to show my real emotions after that, so I hid them behind a thick wall.

No wonder that we struggle to do what we believe is important for us, openly and authentically. Yet, it is only in being fully authentic that we can see what we unconsciously think is important for us and then question ourselves about how these old habits are serving us, what old beliefs we are still dancing to, and how we might want to consider doing things differently. Then we will become open to changing our beliefs and judgments about what we believe *should* be happening. When we stop feeling a desire to judge what other people should or should not say, do, eat, or wear, and how they should or should not act, work, play, or scratch themselves, we will find it much easier to be authentic. Suddenly a virtuous circle will begin to work in our favor.

We will feel much less tempted to be critical or hurtful. There will not even be a hint of criticism in our tone of voice or in our body language, such as rolling our eyes in disgust. By changing our beliefs, we change our heart and our attitude, freeing ourselves to be authentic and present, safe in the knowledge that we will not say or do something with the intention of hurting another person. If others do become offended, we will know that they do so because of their own beliefs and not because we wanted to "stick it" to them. Then we will be able to remain present, true to what's important for us, even if other people are angry with us.

I found that I had to cross many more doorways before I had the courage to be fully authentic most of the time. Gradually, however, my fear that I might say or do something that I would later regret began to dissipate. I found that, increasingly, I could trust what would naturally come out of my mouth. The result was that I became capable of shifting my focus away from worrying about what others would say or do, to one of doing what was right for me and trusting that the real me was *also* what was best for others, even if they disagreed.

Being authentic is when living in the present becomes a "real-world" adventure. You just don't know what will happen next when you are authentic with someone, and when you let them own their own reactions without trying to influence them or to assume responsibility for their feelings. My experience is that my expectations around how others will react to my authentic self-disclosures are wrong nine out of ten times. I simply do not know, nor can I ever know. You may think, "Hah! I know exactly how my spouse or my boss will react." Maybe you do. But maybe you don't. Even if you are right, do they not have the right to experience their own reaction, and to know how you really feel and what you really want?

I now believe that what I owe my life partner more than anything else is to be authentic. This is the one promise that I can keep for a lifetime. I might promise to have and to hold, to love and to cherish till death do us part. But I might not feel that way in ten years. I might not be able to keep that promise without feeling that I am lying to myself. Or without changing who I am in ways that betray and abandon myself. However, that is not true about being authentic. We can promise to be authentic for the rest of our lives. We can promise not to hide our truth, even if our truth feels painful to our partners at times. Being authentic is a doorway to discovering who you really are behind your protective walls, one that faces each of us every day.

Here are some closing thoughts on *Be Authentic*...

Remember...

- You spent years erecting your walls for your own protection. Tearing them down by authentically exposing your truth to others is understandably frightening.
- Role-play-thinking, Replay-thinking, and Fantasy-thinking are ways to alter the present. These thoughts fill our minds and block us from being able to know what's really important for us when we feel uncertain.
- The payoff for being authentic is confidence. You are saying to yourself, "I am worth it. I can trust myself to do what is right for me." Getting there includes claiming your past.
- Important parts of the real you are hidden from your own conscious awareness. You will only uncover these by authentically self-disclosing what you really think and feel.

Watch for...
- Blaming other people for how you feel. Blaming others is the main way in which we are harmfully authentic with others, rather than usefully authentic.
- Trying to control other people's behavior. Much of our over-thinking is geared to trying to influence what other people think of us, or to get them to give us what we want.

Try this...
- Use "I" statements which are linked to other people's actual behavior. "I feel angry that you said my mother wears army boots."
- In a moment of decision, ask yourself: Do I pick me? ...or do I pick the other person? Do I abandon me? ... or do I honor myself enough to do what's important for me, even if others will not like it?

If you have been hiding your truth for years, your becoming authentic can be quite a shock for others. At some point in time, they may even decide that they don't like some of your "authentic" behaviors. This is when doing what's important for you in the moment will become significantly more difficult. Others may impose consequences on you that may feel very hurtful. Now you must learn how to risk the disapproval of others if you want to be fully present and true to yourself in the moment.

Risk Disapproval

GRACE UNDER PRESSURE

If doing what's important now means doing what's right for you, then you must learn how to risk doing so even when it is dangerous. When you hesitate to say or do what you really feel or think, in that moment you are at risk of compromising yourself, of leaving yourself open to regrets and resentment. Perhaps your boss is asking you to stay late, and you had made other plans for the time after work. Perhaps your spouse is wanting you to go with her to visit family, when you would rather just stay home and watch TV. Maybe you are stuck in traffic, having left too late to arrive on time to your appointment, and you just want to scream in frustration. Instead, you pick up the cellphone, call up the person who is waiting for you and tell him a white lie: "The traffic is really bad, Jim. Sorry about that. Can you wait the extra half hour until I get there?" In reality, you know you left too late, but you didn't want to tell him that. That level of authenticity would be too dangerous. Jim might decide that if you are so disorganized, he would be better off doing business with someone else.

When you are authentic, you admit your truth at all times. Your truth is not always something you may want others to know, primarily because they might disapprove of what you said or did. Your boss might get annoyed with you and label you as not being a "team player." Your spouse might get upset with you, giving you the cold shoulder, or make hurtful comments. Your client might not give you the business you want.

As long as it *matters* to us how other people react, we are in danger of deciding to filter, modify, or otherwise change who we are, what we want, and how we will do it. Every time we do this *against our will*, we have betrayed ourselves. When we betray ourselves, we reduce our joy, diminish our excellence, and fuel our need to rehearse what we're going to say, to replay how it went after the fact, and to fantasize about how wonderful life would be if only we didn't have to compromise so much! Our focus becomes divided, and we make it difficult for ourselves to live in the present, doing what's truly important for us in that moment.

On my own journey, I discovered that the belief that lay beneath all my other beliefs was *"I need the approval of others."* Once I understood and accepted this, I found the courage to begin risking the disapproval of others. This was so important because as long as you are motivated by the approval of others, you cannot know with confidence whether the decisions you are making in your life are what's right for you, or whether you are making them with the idea of impressing someone else. If you are out to win the approval of another person, then you have unconsciously linked what you do with getting a specific, positive response from others as a "reward" for doing what they approve of.

If, for some reason, you don't receive what you expect, then you've set yourself up for disappointment, anger, and loss. Risking the disapproval of others is the only way to break this cycle and to begin to know who the real you is and what the real you wants, independently of how other people view your actions.

When the fear of reprisals or the desire for a pat on the back determines what you will say or do, you are letting outside forces influence your decision about what is important for you in a given moment. When you do this, you give away some of your power to external pressures. You are linking your sense of self-worth to whether or not the client chooses you to do business with, whether or not the stock price goes up, the putt goes in, the prospective date says yes, or your husband or wife is happy with you. When you do this while feeling torn inside, you are avoiding your present truth as it really is. Instead, you are trying to alter yourself so that you will get what you *believe* is important now for you. Ironically, you are limiting how joyous the present might be. If you are going to do what's right for you in the present moment, you must develop the inner strength to face the consequences of being true to yourself even if others disapprove. There is no other path to this place of inner strength, though there are many ways to reduce the potential pain and conflict along that path.

Ernest Hemingway defined guts as "grace under pressure." How well we handle the consequences that come our way when we are true to ourselves defines our capability to live in the present. When we are able to stay present even when others respond angrily to our authentic actions, we remain capable of doing what's important for us even under enormous pressure. We respond calmly, consider wisely whether the other person has a valid point, and change our views without hesitation if we feel that this is the right thing to do. Or we stand our ground, in spite of their attempts to pressure us.

Of course, your ability to exhibit "grace under pressure" will be tested when someone seriously disapproves of what you've said or done. When someone is screaming at you, labeling you as lazy, stubborn, and stupid, threatening your job or giving you the cold shoulder for a week, you will quickly discover just how well you are able to stay cool, calm and collected. These are the pressure-packed moments that being authentic can bring on. Learning how to face these crises and still do what's right for you *anyway*, is why it's so important to risk being authentic.

Facing the disapproval of others when you are authentic would be easy if you could count on others to always respond to you with love and support. Ideally, they would be there for you even if the real you were cranky and irritable. If you failed in your career, told your boss to shove it, or broke down and cried in front of fifty people, they would be there for you. If you had an affair, lied about your sordid past, or tried to intentionally hurt someone for your own selfish benefit, they would support you with caring and understanding. What a blissful world that would be!

But this ideal world does not exist that I am aware of, and so you must find a way to separate how you feel about yourself, from the reactions of others to the authentic you. You must find a way to stop viewing their responses to you as being about you. You must no longer view their criticisms or even their compliments as a reflection of whether you are "good enough" in their eyes. Remember, "It's not about me!" To truly own this, you must heal some inner wounds so that you will no longer feel the urge to impress others with how well you are doing, and no longer fear what they will think if you are not a good person in their eyes. You must also learn to stop sending messages, whether subtle or blunt, which let others know that you think they are either not good enough for you or better than you. To risk the possible disapproval of others when you are true to yourself, you must develop a deep trust that you are "good enough," no matter what their response to the real you turns out to be.

I have observed that older people often seem to be more willing to face this risk. Perhaps there is something about having lived a long life that makes them feel more accepting of their own faults. They become willing to say the unspeakable, to do the unthinkable, and to act in a genuine way, whether others like it or not. Having fame and fortune seems to have a similar effect, though not always. Rock star Madonna reveals her sexuality for all the world to see. Basketball player Dennis Rodman is comfortable wearing women's clothes and fluorescent-colored hair. These people give themselves permission to be who they are, whether society likes it or not. Of course, only they themselves know whether they authentically represent themselves to the world, or whether they're putting on an act.

In the end, only you and the universe know whether you were authentic, or whether you put on a protective façade in order to shield yourself and others from dealing with the truth that existed in that given moment. If you choose to be protective, please don't be too critical of yourself. This journey is not easy.

BLAME YOU, BLAME ME

When people use consequences as a way to respond to undesirable behavior in others, they are saying that what happened is somebody's fault. Someone did not do what they were "supposed" to do, and they should be penalized. If children misbehave, they should be sent to their room or have other privileges taken away. If someone insults you, they deserve to be insulted or shunned in return. If the boss thinks you are doing a poor job at work, you should be fired. If a spouse has an affair, their partner is justified in leaving them and in attacking them in whatever way they can strike back at them. A desire to avoid the consequences that come with doing things that others disapprove of is a major factor in why we often don't do what's important now for ourselves.

This fear of consequences that comes when others disapprove of our behavior can be wide and deep. As I became more aware of just how enormous this issue was for myself and for others around me, I began to notice it at several levels. Not only was it true for "hot" issues like getting caught doing something illicit or immoral, it was true on a day-to-day, moment-to-moment basis as well. For example, I went camping with my family one summer. Check-in time for setting up camp was noon. We arrived at our site at eleven o'clock in the morning, only to find another family still on our assigned site. The couple and their three children were patiently sitting on the picnic table, all packed up but with no apparent intention to go anywhere. When I asked them what was happening, they rolled their eyes and said, "We're waiting for those people over there to move so that we can move to their site," pointing to a site just a stone's throw away.

"Oh." I responded. "Have you let them know that you are waiting for them to move?"

"Are you kidding?" exclaimed the husband, giving me an astonished look. "They might bite our heads off! No... they've paid until noon, so we'll just wait until they go."

At that moment, I was struck by how this couple's fear of the other family's *potential* reaction had left them frozen and immobilized. They could not do what they so clearly wanted to do. They were too afraid of the consequences. At some point during their lives, this couple learned that expressing what they want to other people is dangerous. They learned that they must be considerate of other people's feelings, especially if the other person is following the "rules." If they are not considerate, they might get their "heads bitten off." Isn't that how a consequence often feels? The other person is "ripping our head off" with a violent verbal assault on our emotional self.

We learn to seek the approval of others when we are children. Our parents, siblings, teachers, and friends all leave their marks on us. We learn how to adapt ourselves to our childhood environment so that we can avoid hurtful consequences and find ways to feel safe. Understanding how you did this in your childhood can help free you from some of your past-based fears of what others may think or do if you were to be fully authentic.

Some of us were "over-attended" by our parents, who kept a close eye on our behavior and used painful consequences to ensure that we did things "the right way." Sometimes, these consequences were deeply scarring. When I was nine years old, I had a friend named Richie who had such an experience. One day, Richie took off his T-shirt and showed me his back. His back was covered with wide, dark purple welts. I felt sick at the sight. I asked him what happened. "My dad gave me the belt," he answered, rather matter-of-factly.

"Why?" I asked, incredulous that such a thing could happen to a fellow kid.

"I messed up. I was supposed to thin the corn in our garden into little groups of three stalks. I didn't do it right, so my old man took the belt to me." Richie's acceptance of his own "wrong-doing" shocked me even more. He learned in a painful way that doing it the "wrong" way comes with a price. All Richie had to do to avoid the terrible consequences of being beaten was to win the approval of his father. He had to be who his father wanted him to be, not who he really was.

Children of "over-attending" parents learn a very clear and specific set of rules (beliefs) about how things "should" be done. Amazingly, these children develop a kind of false self-confidence. As long as they do it the "right" way, whatever goes wrong must be the other guy's fault. Their tendency to blame others when things go wrong leaves them ill-equipped to be adaptive and flexible in-the-moment.

Others among us had parents who "under-attended" our behavior. They were so busy with their own lives that they barely noticed us. When they did, it was only because we did something "wrong." The effect of this kind of parenting is to rattle the child's confidence, as the child discovers that when they do what they think is right for themselves, a parent-figure is bound to find something wrong with it. Children of "under-attenders" learn to blame themselves for "messing up." After all, whatever they did was of their own volition, without authoritative guidance, and therefore the "mess" they've created must be their own fault. Who else could be to blame? Children who grow up with this style of parenting are hesitant to proceed without first feeling assured that what they are about to do will be approved of by people who matter to them.

The main struggle in striving to do what's important now for you is to overcome your instinctive desire to either blame somebody else or to blame yourself if things don't work out as you had hoped. So long as you feel a desire to blame someone, you will automatically feel a desire to use consequences to penalize either the other person ("What a jerk that guy is!") or yourself for this "bad" behavior ("What an idiot I am!").

This is why self-acceptance is the foundation of living in the present. You must accept that yes, indeed, there may be times when you are insensitive and thoughtless or when you do things the wrong way in your own eyes or in the eyes of others. When you accept your "bad" qualities as sometimes being true of you, you free yourself from the fear of someone critically judging you. You will know in your own heart that you are still a good and lovable person, even though you may have said or done something that, in retrospect, might not have been the "best" choice. When you know that *who* you are is not in question, you will find it much easier to stay present in the face of the disapproval of others to *what* you authentically said or did.

FIGHT OR FLIGHT

Many of us don't have a deep self-assurance about who we are, at least not all of the time. Certainly, I fail regularly. I say something and then I feel self-doubts. I do something and question whether I made a fool of myself. I see what others are doing, and I think they are messing up, not doing it the "right" way as I would have them do it. Every time this happens, I am failing to live fully in the present. Instead, I am judging what is happening in the present against my internal belief system about what "should" be happening. In those moments, exposing your authentic thoughts and feelings is how you see what you *believe* is right for you, even if in retrospect you realize that perhaps you were wrong.

When we blame someone for what is happening, we slip into the two habits that take us away from living in the present. These two habits are so pervasive that we may have trouble seeing them in ourselves at times, even though we might be reacting out of these habits several times a day. These habits are the desire to **fight** or to take **flight** in response to what is happening in the present moment. Both of them are anchored in a desire to take control of the present moment by trying to alter it. When we fight, we are trying to *force* the present moment to be what we want it to be. When we flee, we are *escaping* the present moment, thereby altering it by simply not being there physically, mentally, or emotionally.

There are many ways we can fight in order to change the present. The most common way is to become a bulldozer. We tend to do this in situations in which we feel that we can live with the consequences. Some people do this at home, where they feel their spouse and children will not hurt them. They can come home and be as unhappy and cranky as they want. Over the years, they may have trained everyone to behave as if they walked on eggshells so as not to upset the "bulldozer." Bulldozers create an environment that is largely controlled by them. They get to be pushy and demanding, while everyone else puts up with it, as was no doubt the case in Richie's home.

I was often a bulldozer at work. I used my intellect, my analytical ability, and my willingness to use research to back up my positions. I was also not afraid to be plain old stubborn, though I always had a "logical" reason. I made it hard for people to disagree with me, saying, "*Don't* you think this is the way to go?" I also had a deep-seated belief that I had to be right. I expressed this belief by shaming or humiliating others so that they would feel pressured to agree with me. "What kind of an idea is *that*?" I would say when someone offered up a different proposal. All of these expressions of my disapproval helped me to make sure that my vision and my strategy for how our business should be run would get implemented. Of course, this approach made working for me rather tough! I set high standards, and I demanded results. I monitored my subordinates fairly closely at first, until I was certain that I could trust them to do what I wanted, the way I wanted. Though I got better and better at giving them room to grow, I remained quite tough about which direction we were taking to achieve our business goals, thereby rendering it hard for *them* to be authentic with me if they wanted their performance to be evaluated in a positive light.

Timothy McVeigh, the infamous Oklahoma bomber, also wanted to bulldoze. He wanted to teach the United States government that its citizens would not stand by and be bullied. He was quoted as saying, "It's unfortunate that so many people had to die, but it was the only way that the government was going to get the message." His conviction that the government needed to be "punished" in order to adopt his view of "what's right" gave him the brutal courage to be authentic, blowing up a U.S. federal building, and killing 168 innocent men, women, and children in the process. Needless to say, the terrorists who intentionally crashed the jet planes into the World Trade Center in New York and the Pentagon in Washington were of a similar mindset.

Bulldozing often works really well in the *short* run. If you let others know that you disapprove and you back that up with some serious, tough, and even frightening consequences, they will often give in to you. However, the risk of being authentic in that way is that the recipients will feel angry and resentful. Then they will begin to find ways to get even. They will begin to stall, become uncooperative, and resist what you want sometimes just because it is you who wants it! In the extreme, they might even execute you or begin a war with you.

The second common way to try to change the present moment is to take flight away from it. A common way to do this is to be a pleaser. Pleasers avoid dealing with the conflict of the present moment because they feel scared of what might happen if they were to stand up and fight. They choose to go along with what others want, even if deep down they sense an inner voice that is saying, "This is not right for me!" Pleasing has one terrific advantage: everything that happens to you is someone else's fault. If your marriage is on the rocks, you can blame your spouse, since you always did things their way. If your job stinks, you can blame your boss or your co-workers, since everything was their idea in the first place. If your life is unhappy, you can blame your parents, since you went to the school that they wanted you to attend, and you married the person they approved of. If you were taking action in part to please others, then surely your actions must be partially their fault! What a great source of control this is! We are innocent victims, and they did it to us. Now they owe us. By giving away the power to decide our own fate to another person, we make them responsible, and we can even use guilt to remind them that our unhappiness is their fault. Being a pleaser is a way to build up a reservoir of resentments based on the past. This is a subtle but powerful form of trying to control others by using your arsenal of resentments to produce guilt feelings in the other person so that they will do things your way when you don't like what is happening in the present moment.

There are many other popular ways to "take flight" from the present moment. You can physically walk away from it. You can, for instance, leave the room when tempers get too hot, or leave your marriage when the issues get too overwhelming. You can emotionally avoid the present by pasting a forced smile onto your face when someone says something that triggers you, or by emotionally numbing out when someone is shouting at you or is physically assaulting you. Mentally, your brain can stop thinking logically when a problem seems too complicated or too frustrating, for instance, when there are mechanical or technical difficulties, or when you're dealing with complex business or personal difficulties. In all of these cases, the present moment is not what you want, and you can escape from it, whether or not you are consciously aware that you are doing this.

Whether we fight or whether we take flight, we are seeking to avoid facing the consequences of this present moment. When we fight by imposing consequences on others, we are deciding that what's important now is to have control over others by "making" them do what *we* think is right, regardless of what they think is right. When we flee, we are letting the consequences of others dictate what we think is right for us. We are deciding that what's important now is to feel safe, rather than face the moment as it actually is. The challenge that each of us faces in such moments of conflict is to find the courage to *stay present* in the face of the dangers of rejection, abandonment, and attack from others, rather than fighting or fleeing.

The secret to staying present in the face of the disapproval of others is to heal our *own* desire to use consequences on others. This is a major part of the paradox of learning how to live in the present. When we fully trust that we will not react to the attacks of others, we can trust ourselves to stay true to what's right for us in the face of their punitive consequences. Then we become capable of being the best we can be, totally focused on this present moment without fear that we may do something that we'll regret.

THREE TYPES OF CONSEQUENCES

As you risk the disapproval of others more often, you will begin to recognize what a consequence looks like when it comes your way. By identifying consequences that feel dangerous to you, you will learn how they trigger you and how you can then overcome the fear and anxiety that you feel in reaction to them. Most of the pain and risk of being authentic comes in one of three packages. These are:

1. **Rejection**—People or circumstances do not give you what you want;
2. **Abandonment**—People want to permanently leave you;

3. Attack—People want to physically or emotionally punish you for being "that way."

Let's look at these one at a time:

Rejection occurs when we don't get what we want in spite of our efforts and good intentions. Rejection happens frequently. We ask someone out for a date, and they turn us down. We offer up our best idea at work, and it gets ignored or shunted aside. We invite someone to visit us, and they turn us down. We try to score a goal, and the other team successfully stops us. We buy someone a present and they respond with a yawn, pointing out how they already have three other items like that. We run for an elected office, and the voters choose someone else. Each of these are moments when what we want is being rejected.

How we feel about these rejections depends on what beliefs we have about what is "fair" and "just." We might feel fine that we didn't score the goal we wanted. We might feel embarrassed that the person we asked out for dinner turned us down. We might feel humiliated by our rejection from the voters, or by our friends who don't show up to the party we are hosting.

Rejection can really hurt. My fear of rejection was so great that I often felt inhibited from even *voicing* what I wanted. Asking a beautiful woman out on a date was sheer terror for me. Asking for help from a stranger or to borrow someone else's stuff are two other examples. Any time I felt the odds were against me, I felt hesitant to express what I really wanted. The more my role-play-thinking revealed to me the possibility that I would get rejected, the more I resisted.

When I was rejected, I often felt angry more than anything else. My role-play-thinking had usually convinced me that they *should* agree with what I wanted. My replay-thinking would churn through their words, convincing me that their reasons for rejecting me were not good enough. They were "doing it" to me, and I felt angry and a desire to get even in some way, at some time. The mere fact that I had found the courage to ask for this difficult thing, whether it was a raise, a sexual desire, or something else equally "dangerous" also seemed to fuel my anger. I had to learn how to stop seeing the rejection of what I wanted as being a personal attack.

Abandonment comes when someone rejects us as a person. This happens when others are so upset by our behavior that they do not want to have anything to do with us. Abandonment generally has one condition: we have let others see who we really are, and now they want to run. This could be a work colleague who shuns us, a friend who stops calling us, or a lover who dumps us. No matter how much we try to be different in order to win their approval, they abandon us anyway. This cuts like a dagger, ripping our hearts out, and leaving us feeling worthless and unlovable.

In my youth, I was dumped by two different girlfriends. I opened my heart and soul to these two women, and they responded by leaving me. I felt it could only mean that I, as a human being, was inadequate and unlovable. My fear of abandonment caused an enormous amount of replay-thinking. "What did I do that 'made' her abandon me?" "What did I do wrong?" The more important someone is to your happiness, the more likely you are to compromise what's important now for you by distorting who you really are in order to try to stop them from leaving you.

Oddly enough, this awareness helped me understand why I could occasionally be authentically rude with a waiter, but would feel inferior and overly cooperative with someone who I felt held power over me, like my wife or my boss. I didn't care if the waiter didn't like me and wanted to abandon me. But I did care if my wife or my boss wanted to abandon me. "Not caring" is a way of building a wall around yourself. Of course, caring too much is also a way of having an unhealthy boundary that motivates you to distort who you are and to do things that are not right for you. Eventually, I had to learn how to have one healthy boundary for everybody, rather than crooked boundaries that reacted to my perception of who the other person was or what I wanted to get from them.

Attack comes when someone wants to change us. This person does not necessarily reject what we want, and does not abandon us physically. Mostly, he or she wants to "make" us into the kind of person *they* want us to be. They hope that if they find fault with us, criticize us, or even physically hurt us, we will change. Many of us do this in subtle ways. For example, I became aware that the "authentic" me often used language that was condescending. "What kind of an idiot would do it that way?" was my occasionally menacing undertone. In other words, if you don't do it my way, I will embarrass and humiliate you. Even giving the cold shoulder for a period of time is a form of attack. Using the *threat* of abandonment is an attack designed to "make" the other person change, apologize, or otherwise force them to behave in the way you want them to behave.

We use various forms of these consequences to get others to behave in a way that helps us get what we want. Others use them on us for the same reason. Part of the process of freeing yourself from the fear of the risk of disapproval lies in accepting the fact that rejection, abandonment, and attack are actions taken by other people. How you feel in *response* to those actions is something that is within you and you alone. If you feel angry, frustrated, guilty, or humiliated, then that is your belief system kicking in. Ten people could all get fired by the same company on the same day for the same reason, such as during a workforce downsizing. Five might respond by feeling despair and hopelessness, while the other five might feel as if they had been given a new lease on life. The events and actions of others are not what matters. How you *respond* is what matters if you want to authentically live in the present, filled with the courage to do what's important now for you.

BREAKING THE "PUNCH, COUNTER-PUNCH" CYCLE

When we experience negative consequences, many of us have a strong belief which lets us judge that consequence. We call it being "fair." If Billy took your toy, then you are justified in taking Billy's toy. That's only fair, right? If your spouse left you, then you are justified in sticking it to him or her, right? That's only fair, isn't it, since they were the one who left you. People want to apply consequences in a way that fits the wounds they feel have been inflicted on them. You may have heard of the line from the Bible that suggests we should take "an eye for an eye, and a tooth for a tooth." As I have come to understand consequences, I see that many of us instinctively act this way. I certainly had a deep-seated belief that *"If you hurt me, I will hurt you."* I can probably safely say that I am not alone in this belief. However, I find that if I give pain, I also get pain back. This becomes a vicious cycle of attacks and counterattacks.

We apply consequences to others, both positive and negative ones, for one main reason—to get what we want. One approach we use is to announce our expectations to others so they will know what we want. We let them know that there will be a consequence of some kind if they do not do what we want. How blunt we are about this depends on how "safe" we feel with the person. Personally, I felt freer with someone close, such as my wife, to let her know that I would get angry (a form of attack) if she didn't give me what I wanted. With someone not so "safe," such as my boss, I might just silently dig in and avoid doing what he wanted (rejection). Either way, the message I was giving them was, if you don't do it my way, I will make you regret it.

Punch. Counter-punch. We are trying to get what we want by using pain and fear to control the behavior of other people. We are convinced that if we can just inflict the right amount of pressure, others will change, and we will get what we want. How do you respond to this kind of pressure? Most of us respond by either counter-punching or by caving in, which is another way of saying fight or flight. If we counter-punch, it is because we are afraid that if we don't, we'll just get bulldozed. We aim to teach the other person that we won't stand for their pressure tactics. We want to show them that if they want to play hardball, so can we. Once this cycle starts, the original reason for the conflict tends to get lost. The fight becomes focused on each person's outrage over the most recent wound. The violence in the Middle East is like this. Sure, they may remember why they are fighting. But what really sends tempers flaring is the last bomb and the last three people who were killed. The memory of these tragic losses, now in the unchangeable past, fuels the fever to avenge those deaths.

Was I any different? I was often a pleaser during my marriage. I compromised myself on where I wanted to live, what kind of social life we had, the kind of relationship I had with my own family. I also compromised when I gave up doing my favorite sports and hobbies. I felt criticized for what I wore, how I cleaned up around the house, and what religion I was born with. I let every wound from these compromises fester during the ten years of my marriage until one day, the straw broke the camel's back. I met another woman who accepted my foibles without criticism and who valued what I valued. Within four weeks of meeting her, I left my marriage—suddenly and without warning.

None of my resentments justifies my adultery and abandonment of my wife. I mention them to illustrate that just as when we use consequences on others to get what we want, so will others use consequences back on us. By blaming my wife for my unhappiness and then striking back at her by abandoning her, I stoked the fires of "punch, counter-punch." She responded to my abandonment by counter-punching me. She took legal action, locked up all my financial assets, and severely restricted my access to my son. We set ourselves up for an expensive, exhausting twenty-month legal battle, while at the same time destroying any chance of talking about the real issues in our marriage.

As soon as you get drawn into the "punch, counter-punch" cycle, your ability to live in the present plummets. You risk getting caught up in the battle. You replay the past (they stuck it to me!), and then you fantasize about the future (I'm going to get back at them!). Of course, when you do that to the other person, then you have to be on guard against what they are likely to do to you in return. Then you must live in the future, fearful of the next counter-punch attack that you can expect at any moment.

Using consequences to get what you want is a trap. Your happiness is linked to whether the consequence you use will succeed in *forcing* the other person to give in, stop bothering you, treat you "properly," or behave more kindly. In fact, what you are doing is acting on the belief that getting what you want is in the hands of others. Your sense of self-worth in those moments is linked to the actions and behaviors of others.

You cannot break this cycle of powerlessness unless you yourself stop doing your half of "punch, counter-punch." How can you be spontaneous and decisive, present and at peace with yourself if you are worrying about what nasty consequence someone will throw at you? Instead, your mind will begin to rehearse what you *should* do, or to replay what you *did* do in order to justify your actions. Once you get caught in this vicious cycle, you will find it difficult to know what's important now for you as your mind races with angry thoughts about what did happen, and with fearful thoughts about what might yet happen. Personally, I become especially aware of how this cycle begins when I feel judged by someone. My mind instinctively begins to gather counter-evidence. "Well, you think I'm selfish! How about all those times you wasted money on all your "stuff," turned me down when I asked you to help me, and refused to come with me?" Usually, I can feel my adrenaline instantly kick in and my heartbeat pick up several beats as I unconsciously ready myself for a "fight."

In those moments, we are digging into the past to look for ways to justify our behavior in the face of the how we are feeling judged. The mere presence of these thoughts in our minds is evidence for the fact that we are unsure of who we are and what we did. We are seeking to build a wall to protect ourselves defensively against the attacks of another. If we were confident that we did what was right for us at the time, what would there be to fear? If we were living fully in the present, we would have no problem changing what we were saying or doing in light of new information from the person who is "attacking" us. Yet, the reality for most of us is that this is extremely difficult to do, especially if the disapproval from others feels personal or highly threatening, such as is the case when we feel clouded by the threat of being fired or abandoned in a relationship.

Breaking the vicious cycle of "punch, counter-punch" is further aggravated by the fact that most of us have set up an unconscious pattern of expectations about how we are likely to respond in certain situations. When you react to another person's disapproval, you are teaching them how to get what they want from you. They become *used* to having a certain amount of control over you. They *expect* that you will respond in certain predictable ways when they get angry, withdraw privileges, or even abandon you. When you decide to break the "punch, counter-punch" cycle, you are not responding as expected. By failing to respond, you can expect one thing for sure—they will dial up the consequences! Withstanding that increased pressure from them can be very difficult indeed.

I learned one of my favorite ways to break this cycle from André. This method involves the recognition of the fact that all battles are like a tug of war. One person is pulling on one end of the rope. They want you to pick up the other end. They are throwing the rope in your face by criticizing you or otherwise provoking you by trying to make you feel bad and shamed. You always have the choice to **not pick up your end of the rope**. You can always choose to not be "available" for their attack. You can say, "Thanks for letting me know what you think. I'll let you know what I decide."

The main lesson in breaking the "punch, counter-punch" cycle is that we must stop using punitive consequences as a means for getting what we want. We have to eliminate any desire we have to use even the *threat* of consequences on others. Responding to something that feels hurtful to me without wanting to hurt the other person in return, has meant overcoming some of my most deeply ingrained beliefs about what gives me power. Imagine saying to your spouse that you want something from him or her but that, if they don't give it to you, you will not do anything about it, nor will you feel resentful, even it happens a hundred times. Imagine saying to your child that you want them to clean up their room, and not feeling tempted to say, "And if you don't, I will take away your allowance/not drive you to your activity/not let you have a friend over." Using consequences as a means to get what we want is a deeply ingrained habit for most of us.

Yet the moment you do, the battle is no longer about the clean room. Instead, it becomes a power struggle to show who is carrying the biggest stick. You might win the clean-room battle, but you have taught your child that a person gets what they want by force of power over others. You might convince your spouse into buying that car/ring/trip you really wanted, but you can be sure that he or she will bide their time to use their past "sacrifice" to guilt you into giving them what they want. "Punch, counter-punch" is a one-way ticket to creating a resentful past that sets up future conflict. Both of these take you out of living in the present.

To overcome this lifelong habit, you cannot simply *suppress* your innate desire to counter-punch. Suppressing is the essence of being "politically correct" and is merely a one-way ticket to being inauthentic, leading to more resentful explosions. To live spontaneously in the present, free to have your entire mind, body, heart, and soul centered on doing what is important for you in the present moment, you must find a way to *eliminate* your desire to punch and counter-punch in order to get what you want. Then you will be able to trust yourself to be totally authentic with anyone, anytime, and anywhere. To succeed, you must learn to do what is right for you, without having an underlying intention of trying to change or influence others. They will be affected, of course, and they may even perceive that you *are* trying to harm them. However, you will know in your heart that you are merely doing what is right for you. That is what will give you the courage to be true to yourself when others respond to you with unkind or even punitive consequences. Then you will understand what Mahatma Gandhi called the "joy of suffering." You will be able to endure difficult consequences joyously when you know that you are being true to yourself in spite of how others are responding to you. You will know the deep-seated self-confidence that comes with being true to what's important now for you. How to get to this place of inner strength is what the journey is all about. For now, your main challenge is to recognize a consequence when it comes towards you, and to be aware of how it is influencing what you do and how you think and feel.

Here are a few closing thoughts on *Risk Disapproval*...

Remember...

- We develop grace under pressure when we can let go of our need to win the approval of others. Otherwise, we are merely reacting to our environment, rather than truly doing what is right for us.
- We often seek to blame others or ourselves as a means of trying to alter who they are or who we ourselves are. We must learn to accept ourselves, including our "bad" qualities.
- Fight or flight are the two habits that take us out of living in the present by trying to alter what's happening in the present.
- We must stop our half of the "punch, counter-punch" cycle if we wish to create a safer environment for ourselves through not fueling others to strike out at us.

Watch for...

- Finding a safe way to deal with your past wounds. Probe your beliefs about why you feel angry or resentful, before you explode in anger.
- Letting your dark side lead you to actions you will regret. If you feel you are in danger of crossing serious boundaries, get support. See a therapist, counselor, or a trusted and objective friend.

Try this...

- Recognize the three consequences of rejection, abandonment, and attack. Notice which ones trigger you the most and explore what beliefs these fears are triggering for you. See if you can face those fears anyway.
- Take small risks every day. Dare to tell the bus driver that he or she looks good. Dare to tell the waitress that you are not happy with the service.
- Be easy on yourself when you feel bad or slip in a "dig" at someone. We were all taught at a very young age to use disapproval to get what we want. This is a very difficult habit to break.

When you risk the disapproval of others by being your authentic self in the moment without counter-punching, you open the doorway to doing what is truly important for you, uninfluenced by the fear of reprisals from past wounds. Then you become capable of centering all of your mind, body, heart, and soul on the present moment, making wise decisions and performing any task with excellence and with joy. However, when you fall short of this ideal, you will need to face a new doorway. You will increase your ability to risk the disapproval of others when you reduce the significance of what their disapproval means to you.

Let Go Of Outcomes

A THIRD CHOICE

The approval of others only has power over us if they have something that can hurt us. Therein lies the seductive power of "punch, counter-punch." But we can break out of this cycle by making a third choice. We can let go of those things that give others power over us. We can reclaim our own power by severing our sense of who we are and how we feel, from the people, possessions, and passions that matter to us.

The approval of others only matters if you care. Simplistic as it sounds, it is truth. If you don't care about having relationships with a spouse, children, co-workers, bosses, or friends, no one has a thing on you. If having the right house, a nice car, and enough money for your preferred lifestyle don't matter to you, then someone can fire you anytime they want. Furthermore, if you are indifferent about whether you get the dishes done, lose ten pounds, drive a golf ball straight, or are wearing nicely pressed clothes, then what anyone thinks of your dirty kitchen, your pudgy body, or your lousy golf game matters not one bit. You are free to be the real you, authentic and in the moment, free of worries and regrets. After all, you have no reason to be concerned about what anyone thinks or does!

You can live a very lonely life if you go down this path, indifferent to the cares of this world or the feelings of others. On the other hand, you can live a happy, loving, and very present life if you can break the link between how you feel about yourself and the significance of these people, possessions, and passions. This doorway is about facing the fear that if you let go of the importance of the people, possessions, and passions in your life, you will *give up*. You will stop trying to love the people who matter to you, and then they will leave you. You will stop pursuing the career, the hobby, and the dream home you so passionately wanted, leaving you feeling empty and without purpose. You'll feel rudderless and powerless.

When I left the corporate world for the first time, I was just twenty-five years old. The first thing I noticed when I later phoned someone about a business matter was how indifferent they were towards me. I no longer held a corporate title or wielded the name of a major corporation, both of which had always motivated others to eagerly return my phone calls. Losing that kind of influence hurt, for awhile. When people go through a divorce or the death of a spouse, a similar experience happens. Suddenly, they are no longer "Sue and Bill," or "Mary and Harold." They are just Sue or Bill. They no longer have the "married person" status they once cherished. Changes in parenting relationships that follow divorce are similar. "Dad" is suddenly an every-other-weekend visiting uncle. These are outcomes that matter to us and that often define our sense of who we are.

Letting go of these kinds of outcomes is painful. Few of us eagerly seek this pain because letting go is to risk *losing* these outcomes. Most of us have our losses thrust upon us, against our will. We get fired. We lose a mate. We lose a bundle in real estate or investments. We lose a step in our game, whether it be on the tennis court, in the boardroom, or merely in the home trying to keep up with the avalanche of household chores that awaits us every day. Accepting these losses is what makes letting go a painful doorway.

Yet, there is great joy on the other side of this doorway. The joy comes from discovering that while our fears about people, possessions, and passions going away may come true, we ourselves will still be just fine. We are not our job title, our neighborhood title, or our parenting title; nor are we our image as super-mom, business genius, or fixer of all ailments. We are separate from those outcomes. Once we know this, we become free. The freedom comes from no longer feeling ourselves involuntarily shoot up with adrenaline, heart pounding, palms sweating, and tension headache tightening when any of these outcomes appear to be at risk from out-side forces. Instead, we are calm and focused on what we are doing in the present moment, confident that whether we get the outcome we want or not, we will do what is right for us knowing that there is no risk of losing who we *really* are.

To be fully present, we must feel safe, even if the out-comes we want are at risk. Otherwise, we are irresistibly drawn to live in the future, worrying that we might not get the outcomes, or that we might lose them if we already have them. If we have already lost them, we are lured back to our past memories of how good life was then, and how dark and unhappy life is now. Either way, we are fretting and regret-ting, unable to live fully in the present. Furthermore, the pain of every wound from the past resurfaces each time a situation arises that reminds us of our loss. A young child playing reminds us that we never had children. A lover who threatens to leave us reminds us of the last time we were left abandoned and alone. A casual, cynical remark from the boss triggers fears that our work is not appreciated. Our past becomes a millstone around our neck, darkening our present moment with fears that we may once again face the loss of dreams, hopes, and joys that matter to us.

Each time we felt hurt when our parents disappointed us, our spouse zinged us, or our work aspirations were dashed, we may have put up a wall. "Don't go there," becomes our favorite phrase. We don't want to go back to that painful place, should the present moment appear to be heading in that direction. The result is that we either flee from such moments, or we strike out at anyone who we perceive is trying to "make" us go back to that unhappy place. Fight or flight takes over, and we are incapable of being present and clear-minded about what's important now for us.

We must learn how to let go of our attachment to having a lover, children or a job if we are to be capable of being fully present when these highly desired outcomes are at risk. In doing so, we free ourselves from letting past wounds or future fears numb us out in the present moment. Ironically, we must also learn how to let go of our past joys, lest we fall into the trap of trying to reproduce those joys that once were, but no longer are. These wounds and these joys are no longer real, though their active memories in our minds are major barriers to our ability to see what is now the right thing for us to say or do.

Other people have power over us when they find that we react to these wounds and joys, dangling the carrots of future promises like job promotions and marital bliss, or waving the stick of job loss, career derailment, divorce, or just plain old being upset with us. If you want to achieve the personal excellence that comes with being fully present, you must learn how to let go of the importance of these "carrots and sticks" to you. Then you will be free to focus all of your mind, body, heart, and soul on what's important now for you.

HITTING A BRICK WALL

By definition, letting go means that we are holding on to something. If we have nothing to hold on to, we have nothing to let go of. Therefore, it is serving us to hold on to the outcomes and expectations that we want in life. How are they serving us? By reassuring us that we are doing the best we can...that we are not to blame for what is happening. If we expected the car to start and it didn't, causing us to be late for work, well...we tried to get there on time, didn't we? It was not our fault that the car didn't start. If we expected our spouse to be faithful to us and they are not, then our marriage breakdown was not our fault, was it? If I asked you to get that report done, and you agreed to do it, then when you didn't do it, it was your fault, not mine, right? Each of these situations reflects an expected outcome that will determine who is to blame if things don't work out as planned. Expectations serve us by allowing us to judge ourselves and others in order to explain why the present moment isn't happening the way it should. This allows us to create new beliefs about how the world works and what we must do in order to get what we want. Expectations give us a sense of control, by helping us to predict the future and explain the past in order to get the outcomes we want.

When we are attached to outcomes such as having a job, a family, enough money, a nice home, and good friends, we feel threatened if they are put at risk. While this is totally understandable, these attachments are what motivate us to decide what's important now for us. If the boss hints at reprisals if you don't work late, you might do it rather than keep your date with your spouse. If your spouse gives you the cold shoulder for working late, you might agree to placate him or her in ways that are not right for you. You are, in effect, deciding that what's important now for you is to not rock the boat, because that could lead to losing major outcomes that matter to you.

For me personally, the thought of letting go of the important people, possessions, and passions in my life seemed quite inconceivable. It felt irresponsible, really. I mean, if I wasn't attached to having these people, passions, or possessions in my life, perhaps I would just go sit on a mountain top somewhere and contemplate my navel! What if everybody thought in this crazy way? Wouldn't the whole world fall apart if we all had this "easy come, easy go" view of the world?

Letting go was ultimately about breaking the link between my own sense of self-worth and whether or not I maintained the outcomes that mattered to me. That may be easy to say, but doing it is a tremendously heart-wrenching and painful experience. My attachments and expectations were serving me. If they were serving me, then I was naturally going to feel a loss when I let them go. I felt huge and deep pains when I let go of my attachment to having the experience of parenting my child in a "normal," unbroken family. I was filled with anger and rage at the break-up of my marriage. I felt broken when my good friend Perry died. I had huge hopes and dreams tied up with those people. Those hopes and dreams died when those people were no longer in my life in the way that I wanted them to be. Part of me felt as if I died when those dreams died. The grief is excruciating. The prospect that there could be more of this anguish in my future was frightening to me. My desire to keep that from happening to me fed my fear. That was what I was hanging on to. My fear was that what I did not want to happen, might indeed happen.

We are at our most excellent selves when we let our effort and our intentions be our focus, rather than the outcomes that we hope to get from those efforts. As I increasingly understood the significance of this, I began to recognize just how outcome-focused I was. I reacted angrily if I felt my lover grew distant from me after I had given so much of myself to her. I felt upset at work if my projects were not successful, if my boss didn't notice my efforts, or if my subordinates didn't deliver the results that I expected. I got annoyed with myself if my golf shots went poorly several times in a row, my computer broke down, or traffic was unexpectedly delayed. The outcomes I got as a result of my efforts were a major factor in my unhappiness, inhibiting my ability to feel present, stay focused, and make wise choices. You cannot be "present" while you are angrily or drearily obsessed with the outcomes that are happening to you in a given moment. To know the joy of excellence that comes from being fully present, you have to let go of whether you get what you want as a result of your efforts, efforts which are now in the past.

My therapist, André, once said to me that all of life can be boiled down to two questions:

What do you want? and...

How are you going to get it?

If all of life can be boiled down to those two questions, then letting go of what you want and how you get it is the very essence of letting go. When I was at The Option Institute, our instructor, Bears, offered up the idea that we can want something in a huge way, yet remain unattached to whether we get it or not. I found this to be a mind-blowing concept. Imagine that I could want a happy relationship with my father, yet feel indifferent about whether I got it or not. Imagine that I could want a successful career, a loving marriage, children, money, and so on, and still feel unattached to whether I had them or not. Imagine that I could want to arrive at my meeting on time, have my favorite chair waiting for me at home, have my children clean up their room, hit a golf ball straight, and still feel fine if none of these things were to happen!

When you no longer feel that you *have* to have what you want, your mind becomes open to new ways of getting it. Instead of swelling up with anger at what is *not* happening, you become instantly aware of what the new possibilities are in this new moment. You can call a taxi, pop a frozen dinner into the microwave, clean up the room yourself, sit in a different chair, try a different way to get your children to do their chores, or any of a hundred other possibilities. You can make a new decision quickly, unburdened by the stress and anger of how life is failing to give you what you wanted or how you expected it to happen. When you are able to rise to this level of being present, you will begin to know the joy of excellence through living in the present. You will make new decisions based on new choices that will help you get what you want without trying to bulldoze or please someone because you're not getting what you want. Instead, you become a focused, goal-oriented, flexible person, who is patiently determined to be true to what's right for you!

If you are like me, you will not just snap your fingers and suddenly feel indifferent to whether your marriage succeeds, your career flourishes, or your dishwasher works. If only it were that easy! For many of us, the way we learn how to let go is to have what we want taken away from us. We have to lose the job, face the life-threatening illness, let our marriage crash, and experience the agony of our losses. I call this "hitting a brick wall." Sooner or later, life gives most of us a brick wall—a time when, no matter how hard we try, we cannot get what we want, nor can we make it happen the way we want it done. These are devastating moments. Worrying, fretting, manipulating, pleasing, and bulldozing become useless. Our destiny is not in our hands. Our spouse has died or left us. Our children are misbehaving or dropping out of school. Our career hopes are sinking despite everything we've done to work our hardest and do our best. We have hit a brick wall.

When the outcome you want is not happening, you may feel that you only have two choices—to roll over or to fight even harder. Yet you always have a third choice—to let go. When you let go, you are not giving up. Giving up is precisely the fear that blocks most of us from going through this doorway. There is a better alternative and that is to surrender. To surrender is to remain committed to what you want, but to accept that at present you are not getting it, nor may you ever get it. All you can do is your part. Others will do their part. The outcome may happen, or it may not. That part is out of your hands. Therein lies the true secret of letting go of outcomes. Outcomes are not in your control. The only thing in your control is your effort and your intention. You swing the club—the ball goes where it will. You make the business pitch—the customer decides whether you get the business or not. You request others to help you clean up—they either do it or they don't.

Letting go of outcomes is difficult because we must let go of control. Letting go of control is scary. Yet we have all done it from time to time. When we fly in an airplane, we are surrendering control of our life to the pilot, the aircraft, the uncertainties of the weather and even the possibility of being hijacked. People who have a fear of flying feel afraid because they know that for those few hours, their lives are completely out of their control. If the plane begins to crash, there is not a single thing they can do except to start praying. Yet with time and experience, most of us learn to trust the pilots, the planes, and the weather. Statistically, in fact, flying is a far safer way to travel than driving or walking, yet few of us become white-knuckled on our way down the street! We feel in control when we are driving or walking, even though we are actually in more danger, demonstrating how our emotions can unconsciously override our intellect.

The first time I went to court in my divorce battle with my ex-wife, I felt that same kind of white-knuckle fear. I was not in control, and I knew it. I couldn't even speak a word in my own defense. Only my lawyer was allowed to speak on my behalf. Certainly, the judge was not in my control nor open to my influence. I felt frightened because whatever he decided would seal the fate of my financial well-being and my access to my young son. Much as I hated the feeling, I was forced to accept in a painful way that I did not have control. But at no time did I stop passionately wanting my goals—access to my son and my share of our money.

Suddenly, I felt a little bit freer. I prepared my case with my lawyer as best as I could. After that, there was nothing more I could do. Over time, I discovered that there was a comfort in relying on a judge to make decisions for my ex-wife and me that I came to like. I didn't have to argue or manipulate her. Neither did she have to do the same with me. We each just did our best and let the cards fall where they may. When you let go, life becomes an adventure, and you learn how to play it one moment at a time, to the limit of what is within your control and not one inch more.

Hitting a brick wall is one way to discover the painful

truth that you are not in control of the outcomes in your life. This is no different in principle, whether you are robbed, whether your health is unexpectedly damaged, or whether someone dear to you dies. All of these are ways in which something that you cherished dearly, was ripped away from you. At that moment, you are faced with the stark reality that you are indeed not in control of the important outcomes in your life, even if you want to be. You can't make a thief return your missing goods any more than you can raise someone you love back from the dead.

Letting go of outcomes is frightening because we must accept how powerless we are over outside factors in our lives. Yet, letting go of them is precisely what gives us the freedom to focus all of our mind, body, heart, and soul on doing that which we can control—our efforts and our intentions relating to what is happening *now*. When we are no longer semi-paralyzed with anger or fear that the outcomes we want are not happening, we become capable of dramatically increasing our ability to find new and innovative ways to make them happen anyway. We become willing to persevere to much greater lengths because our sense of well-being is not tied to the instant gratification of getting what we want right now. Instead, we learn that what's important now is to do what is right for us, regardless of how many times we've been defeated, how many obstacles appear before us, or how much some people may disapprove of what we are doing. When we do this without using "punch, counter-punch" to intentionally strong-arm others, we become powerful human beings indeed. We are choosing to not control what life is giving us. We are ceasing the struggle. We are accepting that if the carpet gets wrecked, it gets wrecked. If we are late, we are late. If we get fired, we get fired. If our marriage dissolves, it dissolves. If we die, we die.

Yet we are not giving up. We can still want a clean carpet, a good job, a loving spouse, and a long, healthy life. It's just that when we are present, our sense of well-being is not linked to whether we have them or not. Learning to live our lives in the present is to learn to separate ourselves from the world around us. Paradoxically, the end result of doing this is that we then feel free to be fully connected to that world. To be present is to be separated and connected all at the same time.

EXPECTATIONS

Many of the outcomes we have focused on so far are oriented to what we want—the people, possessions, and passions in our lives. Painful as these are to let go of, there remains a subset of outcomes that is even more pervasive for most of us and equally difficult to let go of—our expectations. As you become more present, you will notice that your barrier in many ways is not found in the big outcomes that you want, such as your house, your spouse, or your job. Letting go of these very important outcomes will most certainly reduce the underlying causes of your replay, role-play, and fantasy-thinking, but these big outcomes are rarely threatened on a day-to-day basis. True freedom to live fully in the present comes when you also let go of the day-to-day outcomes that you want. I call these "expectations."

Our expectations are mainly our beliefs about *how* we are supposed to get what we want on a "moment-to-moment" basis. Expectations are happening in virtually every moment of every day. We expect our computer to work, our paycheck not to bounce, our appointments to happen on time, our dog to return home, our lawnmower to start, our spouse to be supportive, our children to do their homework, and so on. All of these moment-to-moment outcomes are generally linked to the bigger outcomes that we want. If your husband is constantly making hurtful remarks, perhaps he wants to leave you. If your computer doesn't work, perhaps your assignment will be late, your boss will be unhappy and you will hurt your career prospects. If your children don't do their homework, perhaps that will lead to poor study habits, weak grades, and dropping out of school—even if your kids are only in grade two right now! Expectations are the pre-conceived notions from our past of *how* things should be done, in order for us to get *what* we want.

Expectations are what we use to *compare* and *judge* the present moment. If reality does not measure up, our expec-tation becomes a reason to become unhappy in some way. Our mind becomes preoccupied with the annoyance, the injustice, and even the outrage that our expectations were not met and might never be met. Our broken expectations motivate us to fight in order to force our expectations to be met by setting the world straight. Expectations also motivate us to flee in order to avoid the conflict that we expect would come if we tried to enforce our expectations on others.

Expectations are happening in almost every moment. When you get on a highway wanting to arrive at your des-tination on time, you probably want to travel at full and normal speed. When the traffic gets backlogged, you might get frustrated. Perhaps you catch yourself and decide to change your expectations instead of getting frustrated. Perhaps you decide that you will allow one hour instead of the usual thirty minutes that this trip normally takes. Well, I don't know about you, but when that hour is up and I am still crawling my way into the city, I begin to feel even more frustrated and angry. I can't be the only one out there, because there is a lot of road rage happening on our North American highways.

When I wake up in the morning hoping to do some important outdoor activity, such as golfing, and it is pouring rain, my expectations are not being met. For a moment, I feel annoyed. I might respond by making a critical comment about the weather reporter. "Those weather people always get it wrong!" Sometimes I'll think it's about me. "Why do I always get the worst weather when I want go golfing?" In some way, I am seeing the bad weather as a reflection of me, as if I am just an "unlucky" person who "never" gets the outcomes he wants. When my spouse says she'll clean up the garage, and a week later it's still not done, I might feel ticked off. What is the matter with her? Doesn't she care whether or not I can park my car inside? Doesn't she realize that her inconsiderate behavior is *forcing* me to be late because I *have* to brush the snow and ice off my car every morning?

Each and every moment of every day, we are holding a set of expectations about what should be happening, and we are comparing it with what is actually happening. Each time that we do this, we are not being present. Part of our mind is occupied with the thought: "This is not right...!" Then we get occupied with our emotional reactions about what *should* have happened: "Argh-h! I want to wring that guy's neck for telling me to go to this useless meeting!" In those moments, our ears, our eyes, and our minds are partially closed. Then when someone asks us what happened, we wonder why we can't remember the details. Of course, we can't! We weren't entirely there. Our mind was off rehearsing what we are going to say to that guy the next time we see him, reducing our ability to be clear-minded about what is right for us in this present moment.

Personally, I was not just a rank amateur about having expectations. I was a professional! I went out of my way to set expectations. I had a deep belief that I *had* to have expectations. My business training had taught me that one must always have a goal in mind, a standard to achieve, a measure by which to know if I and my business were successful. I used to measure the time it would take me to get anywhere and then judge how well I was doing compared to my best time. I could feel the adrenaline course through my body as I measured my time and progress, motivating me to dart in and out of traffic in the hope that I would achieve my time standards. I created elaborate spreadsheets that measured my savings, my investments, my returns, and my expectations about how soon I could retire, depending on how much money we had and how great the returns were.

My ex-wife and I had an enormous number of expectations about how we should each behave if we were to be considered a "good spouse." Whether we got each other the right kind of gift, said the right kind of words to each other about the gift, or said the right thing about the other's appearance or work achievements. For virtually everything, we had an expectation about what was right and wrong behavior. These expectations ultimately defined whether we really "loved" each other. Little did I know how far removed from love it was, to burden each other like that. We could not accept the other person as we each really were. Our expectations blinded us to seeing and appreciating the good that was in each of us, as we busily judged each other's shortcomings during and after our marriage.

Expectations provide the fuel to justify the "punch, counterpunch" cycle. We become convinced that the missed birthday card, the forgotten pat on the back at work, and the careless snide remark that hurts our feelings, are each powerful pieces of evidence that the other person doesn't really care, doesn't really love us, and doesn't want to be helpful to us. If they are doing that to us, well, then surely we are justified in doing it back to them the next time they want us to be helpful or thoughtful. After all, if we don't respond to them in some appropriate way, like attacking (a subtle dig), rejecting (being uncooperative), or abandoning (ignoring them for a couple of days), how are they going to learn? In those very moments, we have stopped being present and true to what's right for us. We are letting a wound from the past, however slight, infiltrate the present moment and influence what we would normally want and how we would normally go about getting it if we were simply being true to ourselves. We are deciding that what's important now is to get that other person to behave differently!

If you want to make wise decisions in the present, you must learn how to let go of your unmet expectations and decide what you now want in light of this new reality. What's more, you must do so without an intent to counter-punch and without repressing a desire to counter-punch, which is merely a way to build up resentments that will come back to haunt you later. This is a difficult challenge. Your motivation must come from the gratifying sense of joy that you will feel when your unmet expectations no longer measure your sense of self-worth nor spin you into an unhappy place.

Four Ways to Let Go

One way to let go is to hit a brick wall, as I have already mentioned. This is the reactive, painful, only-deal-with-it-if-you-have-to way to let go of outcomes. Even if you have that route thrust upon you, it does not guarantee that you will let go. People have been known to hang on to resentments about past hurts for years, like those who have suffered trauma, family tragedies, or divorce. People will pursue dreams that have passed them by for years as well, like athletes who just "don't have it" anymore, or managers who can no longer keep up the pace yet desperately want to hang on to their positions.

If you want to break out of some rut in your life, you must learn how to proactively let go. There are a number of ways that can open this doorway for you. Before I go there, however, I want to remind you that the key to success is that you must begin to see how the rewards of letting go exceed the benefit of staying stuck where you are. If you find that letting go seems impossible, it will be because whatever you are hanging on to is serving you in some way, even if that payoff is not available to your conscious mind.

One approach to letting go is to look at the worst-case scenarios. You start by recognizing that you are attached to certain outcomes. Then you consider just how bad things would be if you were to lose them. You must find the courage to look these possible losses squarely in the eye, allowing yourself to feel the pain that you will likely feel at the prospect of losing something near and dear to you. I once was in the habit of not wanting to look at these "worst-case" scenarios. For example, I did not want to discuss with my first wife what we would do if one of us were to die, or to leave the marriage. Somehow I thought that talking about it would make it happen, and that being ready for it would accelerate its arrival. Instead, I unconsciously developed a huge fear over time that I would not be able to survive if something ever happened to her. This fear left me feeling controlled by her, motivating me to resentfully give in to her wishes on important outcomes like lifestyle, family relationships, and career decisions.

Facing your fears is much more than merely having an academic debate in your mind about whether you can live without your job, your spouse, your child, your money, and so on. You must actively explore exactly what you would do if the outcome you so desperately want to avoid, happened anyway. Do you trust that you'll find another job, another love partner, another house, another treasured keepsake? Do you trust yourself that you will be okay if someone attacks or abandons you if you decide to be true to what you think is right for you? When you feel satisfied that you can see how you will survive and even thrive if these worst-case events happen to you, you will begin to free yourself of their power over you. Certainly, the ability of others to "pressure" you using rejection, attack, and abandonment will dramatically decline when you accept that you can live with those punitive consequences.

Then you know that you always have a choice. You can risk letting your child walk to school by himself. You can risk that your spouse will leave you if they think that the real you, with your own true feelings, habits, and preferences is not "good enough" for them. You can chance it that your client will fire you, or that your colleagues will sabotage your career if you say what you really believe is right for the company. You can trust yourself that you will not fall apart if your worst fears arise and your child is hurt, your spouse leaves you, or you are fired. You can take the risk of letting go if your Inner Knowing is in conflict with getting or keeping the people, passions, or possessions to which you are attached.

This is asking a lot, especially if you have to let go of everything all at once. But in the present moment, these losses will not happen all at once. In fact, many of them may not happen at all. It is our *fear* that we will lose something of value that is often blocking us from being present, flexible, and adaptive. It is our *fear* that our past dreams will not happen that blocks us from doing what is important for us now, as we try to force the future to unfold the way we believe it should.

A second way to let go is by accepting a new belief: life is not fair. Even if you pour your heart and soul into your job, your kids, your marriage, and your physical health, any one of these may crush you with disappointment at any time. No matter how hard you try, no matter how much talent, beauty, money, or friends you have, you still might not get what you want. Life is not fair, and that can really hurt. I met an older divorced woman in one group I attended who was still hanging on to a great deal of anger and resentment towards her former husband, eight years after their divorce. She bemoaned the lost "easy retirement" that she had expected to spend with him after having been married for more than thirty years. Now she was living alone in a much more modest lifestyle. She had neither expected nor wanted this outcome and felt that she deserved more. Her focus was on blaming her ex-husband for her situation. She could not let go of her expectations about what life was *supposed* to give her. In her mind, she did everything right. She had children, attended his work functions, kept a clean house, and cooked good meals. She "followed the rules." Yet she still did not get what she wanted. She could not let go of the unfairness of it all, even eight years later.

I sympathize with her. Certainly, she has to grieve her losses for a time. However, someone in her position will recover much faster when she realizes that she is grieving a fantasy. She never had the easy retirement in the first place. All she had was her expectation, a past dream to which she was deeply attached. When she accepts that, she will have the opportunity to see her new "present" and decide how to make the most of it. I don't think it will be a coincidence that the odds of new relationships and new financial opportunities will increase dramatically for her. Being present means being at peace with what is. When we are at peace with our present circumstances, life has a funny way of beginning to re-build. But that is only a hope, not a guarantee.

A third way to let go is to ask yourself, "Do I really know that having this person or possession in my life is what is best for me?" I had the incredibly good fortune of achieving much of what I wanted at a relatively young age. The greatest benefit of that has been the awareness to me that what I wanted did not make me as happy as I had thought it would. I have no reason today to think that just because I expect something to be terrific, it will be that way. I have no reason to think that just because I expect something to be awful, it won't turn out to be terrific in some unexpected way.

I used to believe that I would be miserable if I were alone and no longer married. The opposite proved to be the case. I could only accept my aloneness after my divorce by letting go of my attachment to having a love partner. I used to feel that I would explode with frustration and anger if my divorce case did not get settled quickly. I learned that I had the staying power to stick with it for years if that would have been necessary. I just had to discern the right reasons for persisting and to know that my motive was not to punch or counter-punch my ex-wife, but rather to do what was right for me. Then I was able to let go of my attachment to whether it ended quickly or not and to focus on what I wanted—access to my son and my share of our frozen assets.

A fourth way to let go is to "Be Grateful." Being grateful helps you to let go by appreciating what you do have, and knowing that you will be fine with just that. This is the basis for the "positive thinking" messages that you have undoubtedly heard many times over the years. Being grateful is extraordinarily powerful. You can be stuck in traffic and be thankful that you have a good car. You can have a computer breakdown and be thankful that you have the ability to operate it, even if you can't fix it. You can imagine what life would be like without your cranky spouse, your noisy children, or your annoying parents and then appreciate them anyway.

Yet being grateful is extraordinarily difficult. You can feel as if you are ignoring and even invalidating your anger or your resentment. To succeed in letting go by being grateful, you must learn how to release your angry or resentful feelings so that these emotions are truly gone, and not just swept under the carpet simply because you've "decided" to be grateful. It has been my experience that, until you learn how to do this effectively, being grateful doesn't really work any more than remembering the starving people in Africa will relieve you of your annoyance with a bad meal at a restaurant. We will look at how to let go of these feelings in the next chapter.

The measure of whether you have truly let go will be the extent to which you can put the outcomes that you want at risk. This is only significant in those moments when you are torn between being authentic and true to yourself versus giving in to what others are pressuring you to do. Only you will know in your heart whether your attachment to the outcomes and expectations in your life is actually stopping you from doing what's important now in order to feel centered and at peace with yourself. You will know if you are kidding yourself because you will feel filled with doubts or resentments. When you are fully present, your Inner Knowing will be the little voice within that will guide you towards doing the right thing for you. The ultimate challenge in being present to that degree is to feel confident that you are connected to your Inner Knowing, and not letting your logical thinking or your feelings unduly influence what you ultimately decide to do.

Facing our fear of losing what we care most about is the best way to reduce the likelihood of these losses actually occurring. Dr. Viktor Frankl, psychiatrist, holocaust survivor, and author of *Man's Search for Meaning*[5], calls this "paradox-

---

[5]*Man's Search for Meaning*, Dr. Viktor Frankl, 1946

ical intention." He says that we must learn how to laugh at our fears. When we are free of our fears, then we will find the happiness and inner confidence that comes with being our real, authentic selves. This is the paradox in letting go: it is only in being willing to risk losing what you have that you will really ever be able to "have" it in the end. If you are very afraid of losing an outcome that deeply matters to you, you will actually create the conditions that will enable your fears to be realized. In other words, you cause yourself to lose the very thing that you fear losing. Your nervousness about how well you will give a speech, make a putt, perform on a first date, or host a social dinner, actually hinders your ability to be at your height of excellence, thereby putting at risk the very thing you want—the applause, the low score, the new love partner, the good impression on your guests. Sure, you might survive, and perhaps you will even get away with it. But you will know yourself that you were not at your best and that you did not feel as good as you wanted to while you were doing it.

This fear of letting go often appears in love relationships. After my separation from my wife, I was dating a woman who attracted me with her open and vivacious personality. Then, as I got emotionally closer to her, her fear that I would find her to be inadequate led her to withdraw, paradoxically pushing me away. When I felt angry and then withdrew in response to her withdrawal, she used my actions to justify that she was correct in withdrawing because I was clearly seeing her as unlovable. We were both on the same treadmill, wanting love yet fearing it, pining for it yet pushing it away at the same time.

Letting go is an emotionally draining and frightening experience. To say anything less would be misleading. We are letting go of control. I believe that, until the day we die, we will always be faced with letting go. Our dream job will fade as our work changes and our favorite co-workers leave. Our dream home will change as our children grow up, the house becomes a bit cavernous, and the neighborhood evolves. Our love relationship will change as our sexy lover becomes a middle-aged person. Our day will unfold differently than we planned it to be. That golf shot that you planned to hit over the pond may land right in the water. Each loss hurts, no matter how big or small. Yet there is joy and peace that comes with knowing that you are okay, even if you don't get what you want or how you wanted it. Your burdens are fewer and your happiness is greater.

WHO IS IN CONTROL?

When we have the people, passions, and possessions that we want, we feel safe and in control. We think that if we are pretty enough or handsome enough, people will want to be with us. If we have enough money, we'll get to belong to social groups that we admire. If we are rich enough, successful enough, have a good-enough family with good-enough children, and good-enough athletic and social skills, then people will like us and respect us. I used to fantasize about how, if I had lots of money, everybody would want to be my friend, even if they disliked me. Somewhere deep inside myself, I had a fantasy that went like this: "Boy, when I'm so successful, then they'll really come crawling to me." Having people, possessions, and passions are ways of enticing and even forcing others to give us their love and respect. Letting go of these is to lose control, leaving us with no other choice but to do what we can for ourselves and accept whatever life gives us in response. Of course, this is precisely what gives us the power to be the best we can be, free from worries and anxieties about what might happen or should have happened.

Let's say you live up to this lofty ideal. You truly let go of all outcomes and focus purely on the process and on the intention that you have in doing whatever you are doing. Then an outcome of some kind happens. You buy stock and it goes up or it goes down. You marry someone, and he or she loves you or leaves you. You work hard and your project is successful or it's not. You plan a summer party and the weather cooperates or it doesn't. How do you explain to yourself why you got the outcome you got? At some level, most of us want to know "why me?" You cannot fully let go until you come to some kind of peace within yourself that explains who is in control and, therefore, why you are or are not getting what you want. Otherwise, you will find it very difficult to let go.

There are four sources that explain who is in control of whether you get what you want. They are:

1. Other people
2. You yourself
3. Fate
4. A Higher Power

Whether you get what you want or not is to the credit or fault of one or more of these. Blaming one of these four through replay, role-play, or fantasy-thinking is what often takes us out of the present. To fully let go, each of us has to come to peace with whomever or whatever we think is in control, for not giving us what we expected and felt we deserved. Let's look at each one of these four sources of control:

The first is **Other People**. Other people can reward you in many ways. They can open career doors. They can invite you to social events. They can admire your accomplishments. They can just be there for you, giving you a shoulder to lean on and a hug when you need one. They are in control of those outcomes. They can give you what you want...if they like you…if they approve of you. If not, then…they won't. Then, if you don't get what you want, it is their fault.

A second one is **You yourself**. You are the one who is in control of getting the outcomes that you want. If your career blossoms thanks to your hard work, it was you who did that. If your investments take off thanks to your wise decisions, it was you who did that. If you win the lottery, it was because you were smart enough to buy a ticket. You won because you earned it. You are in control of what happens to you. Of course, if your career fails or your investments lose value, or if you always lose while gambling, it was also you who was in control. Bad you. Then these terrible outcomes are all your fault.

The third one is **Fate**. Some people call this "lady luck." Some people call it "that's life." If you decide to put some money in a small company and the stock market takes off, you make a fortune. No one did it for you. You just laid down your money and bingo, you're a winner! If you decide to go to a party and you meet the mate of your dreams, you're a winner again! You date, you fall in love, you marry…it was all just good luck and fortunate timing. Of course, your dream date could turn into your divorce nightmare. Your investment could go sour and you could lose a lot of money. Then what? Then you got unlucky. You took a risk. That risk might have paid off or it might not. You don't know whom to blame. It's just random luck. It's hard to blame fate. For that reason, fate seems to always lead back to YOU. You have bad luck because you are not lucky or special. You were born under the wrong star at the wrong time. So really, it is not fate that is in control. It is still you. Perhaps it is your very existence as a bad and unlovable person that is bringing you all this bad luck.

The fourth and final "something" that could be in control of giving you what you want is **A Higher Power**. The universe. God. This higher power could have decided that you deserved to win a million dollars in the lottery. "He" could have decided that your spouse should die. "He" could have decided that you will have the talent that you have. Other people did not do these things to you. You certainly didn't do these things to yourself, did you? Maybe it was just a coincidence or random luck. Maybe the first time. But not by the fifth time. No, by then it must have been an intentional decision made by a higher power. If the outcome is positive, then God must think that you are pretty special. If the outcome is negative, well, then God must not think too much of you. Then you can be angry with Him. It is His fault that things are not going your way.

Letting go means figuring out whom you are blaming and then letting go of that. I think that all of us believe that someone or something *has* to be in control. If not, then life is a series of random chances. Then you are left with the prospect that your life is like living in a rudderless dinghy tossing about in the middle of the ocean. Whether you survive or thrive amid the jagged icebergs and ferocious storms is completely out of your hands. I think that when people feel suicidal, this is how they are seeing their lives. No one is in control, and life is just a series of unexpected and random disasters that leaves them feeling very afraid of life. They would rather give up than face that prospect on an ongoing basis.

If you want to let go of trying to control what happens in your life without giving up on life itself, then you must choose who is in control. Personally, I have decided to believe that God is in control. I believe that He knows what is happening to me and is deciding to allow certain events to happen in my life that are, in some often unknown way, good for me. I believe that He wants me to be authentic, and to listen to the Inner Knowing within me. I believe that if each of us did this, the result would be that we would each be fulfilling our true destinies. That means that if someone rejects what you want, then what you wanted may not be part of your destiny. Then again, maybe it is. Maybe you are meant to persist and persevere. The only way you can really know is by listening to your Inner Knowing. The only way you can hear that voice is to be as present as you can be, fully connected to your physical, emotional, mental, and spiritual self.

Our Inner Knowing knows what is truth for us. We must find and follow that voice, letting go of the ego battles in which we try to control what happens in our lives by "punch, counter-punch." Yet we must persist where conflict is in the way of our purpose. Either way, we are at peace because the cooperation we are getting or the conflict coming our way is not a reflection of us. Rather, they are just what is happening. Now we become free to decide what's right for us, in this new moment, rather than deciding what's important now based on our past expectations about what life *should* have given us.

There is another belief that helps me to embrace this notion that a higher power is in control: *Every cloud has a silver lining*. This is so old and so time-worn that it almost goes in one ear and out the other. But stop for a moment. Terry Fox has cancer, loses his leg, runs across Canada, dies, and leaves behind a legacy that raises tens of millions of dollars every year for cancer research. The death of Terry Fox is a cloud. But what a silver lining he has left behind!

When I was working with my therapist during my divorce, I cried out my grief around the loss of the many hopes and dreams that my wife and I used to share that would no longer come to pass. He would say to me, "You will have those same hopes and dreams again. It just won't be with her." There will be a silver lining. We just have to look for it. We just have to wait for it. We may never even know what it is within our own lifetime. We simply have to trust that the loss we are grieving will somehow bear positive fruit.

Dr. Viktor Frankl survived more than three years in a Nazi concentration camp during World War II. Fewer than one in twenty people survived that horrific experience. As a psychiatrist, he made this observation about what separated those who survived from those who did not. "We had to learn ourselves and, furthermore, we had to teach the despairing men *that it did not really matter what we expected from life but rather what life expected from us.*"[6]

Letting go means trusting that "Life" is giving you what you are supposed to be receiving, even if it is not what you *want* to be receiving from Life. I translate "Life" in my mind to "God." Our higher power is giving us the experience He wants us to have, even if it is not the experience that we want to have. This does not mean that we do not make our own decisions. Rather, it means accepting that we are not in control of what happens after we have done our part. The outcomes we get happen with God's permission.

I don't believe that you have to "make" yourself let go. Letting go is really about making a choice *in the moment* when you are faced with the very real possibility that you might lose something to which you are attached. If your job is good, why try to force yourself to emotionally let go of it? Facing your fear of letting go of your job is worth pursuing only if you are aware that your attachment to the income, the status, or to how good you are at your job, is holding you back from doing something that you suspect is right for you. Then your attachment to your job is probably blocking you from hearing and acting on your Inner Knowing, leaving you in danger of having to bury part of yourself in order to drown out that voice. Your risk is that this submerged part of you will re-emerge in the form of physical aches and pains, emotional stress, and mental cloudiness.

---

[6]Man's Search for Meaning, Dr. Viktor Frankl, 1946, 98

How to let go is therefore about making a choice to face your fear in the moment, rather than choosing to postpone or avoid it. You are deciding to *risk* the loss of your attachment and trusting that you will survive *if* the loss occurs. Your inner strength will grow each and every time that you feel the inner conflict between being authentic versus being protective, and you choose to do what is right for you without the desire to punch or counter-punch.

Leonardo DaVinci was quoted as saying, "I thought I spent my whole life learning how to live. Instead, I discovered that I spent it learning how to die." When we die, we face our final letting go. We let go of life itself. That is the ultimate letting go. Coming to peace with dying is an important way for us to learn to live our present life at peace. Then we can begin to truly trust that whatever is happening in this present moment, we will handle it.

Here are a few closing thoughts on *Let Go of Outcomes*...

Remember...
- Your attachments are the results that you want in life. If they are linked to your sense of self-worth, they can become the barriers to knowing what is important for you.
- Having your attachments ripped away from you does not mean that you've actually let them go.
- Letting go of expectations opens you up to new possibilities which could be even better than you expected.
- Letting go happens when you act in a way that reflects your genuine decision to put your attachments at risk.
- Your "Inner Knowing" becomes available to you when you surrender, without giving up. Then you will discover what you are really capable of achieving.

Watch for...
- Convincing yourself that you don't want something, when really you do.
- Stubbornly clinging to attempts to make other people do it "your way" or the "right way."

Try this...
- Think of a major struggle in your life. Then ask yourself who is controlling the outcome that you want. Can you find a way to imagine that what that person is doing is in some way good for you?
- If you feel a desire to counter-punch someone, ask yourself, "What would I do if I felt indifferent towards this person?" Then try doing it, just to see what it feels like to let go.

Letting go is the antidote to needing the approval of others. You will begin to trust that somehow, what is happening in the present moment will sooner or later be good for you. Once again, however, there is a doorway blocking your progress. It is called Feel Your Feelings. So long as you remain afraid of the intensity of your emotions that most assuredly come with letting go, you will remain blocked from truly doing it. How can you trust yourself to act spontaneously and wisely in the moment if you feel afraid that your angry or frightened feelings might suddenly explode out from you? You must learn how to grieve your losses, fully and completely, in order to let go of hurt feelings and return to living fully in the present, emotionally centered, and capable of performing with excellence.

Feel Your Feelings

GRIEVE YOUR LOSSES

We cannot let go of the past enough to live in the present unless we are able to grieve our losses. We must deeply feel our emotional pain in order to accept that what is happening in this present moment is not what we wanted. Then we can let go of those past dreams, return to the present and do what's important for us to feel centered, strong and confident. Then all of our mind, body, heart, and soul will be focused on the new choices and the new opportunities in front of us, even if they aren't the ones we had hoped for.

Feeling your feelings is to stop injecting the freezing. It is to feel the fear of what your life is like now that you have lost someone you loved, a job you enjoyed, or a possession you treasured. Will you be okay? Can you handle it? What if you collapse and crumble into a state of inert depression? What if you strike out in rage at the persons who caused you to lose what you so dearly valued? If you don't fully grieve your losses, the wounds from your crushed dreams may well fester within you, magnifying the intensity of how you feel and limiting your ability to deal with present-moment crises and pressure. The previous times that you felt hurt by a rejection, an attack, or an abandonment, will spring back into your memory, magnifying your present sense of danger and leaving you much less capable of hearing and understanding what is actually happening in the present moment. Such is the power of your feelings. Your feelings can be your best ally or your worst enemy. Mastering them so that they work *for* you rather than *against* you, can unleash your ability to perform with excellence in the moment.

Every sports fan knows that when the chemistry is right on the team, the ability of that team to perform to its highest levels is dramatically accelerated. Every business manager knows this to be true for his or her organization as well. When people feel emotionally connected to each other and to the goals of their group, they work together better, overcome obstacles more effectively, and feel good about themselves. Couples know this to be true, too. When they feel loving and supportive towards each other, day-to-day bumps and crises are handled with ease, with flexibility, and with understanding. Feeling emotionally connected and centered is a well-known part of any "success" formula touted over the years by various motivational speakers and human potential gurus.

The key to tapping into this wellspring of personal excellence begins with grieving your losses. Unless you can effectively grieve your losses, you will be left with a tender spot inside you that will hold back part of your passion. You will automatically build a wall to contain that wound, which will protect you from feeling the intensity of its pain, and will stop you from wearing your wound in public. But the wound will remain nonetheless. When you grieve your wounds, you heal them so that you re-emerge as resilient, flexible, and capable of dealing with unexpected crises, disappointments, and even crushing losses with wisdom and compassion. You become a tower of strength.

While most of us are familiar with the great joy of feeling emotionally connected, purposeful, and passionate, we tend to rely on others to create that experience for us. When I left my job after my "magical" time with the first company that I worked for, I sought to reproduce that feeling by finding another job with a similar company and similar people. I tried three different career moves in less than two years before I found a situation in which I felt comfortable. When I broke up with my first girlfriend, I sought to reproduce the deep feelings of love that I had felt for her, in a relationship with another woman. If I didn't feel that same magic relatively quickly, I gave up and moved on. For several years, I did not date at all. I poured myself into my work. I felt discouraged at times that life was not giving me what I wanted in order to feel *satisfied* with my life.

When you grieve your losses, you create for yourself the ability to feel centered and at peace with what is happening, no matter what has happened in the past. I had an instructor who described how she tried twenty-seven different ways to motivate her daughter to clean up her bedroom. Each time that this mother tried and failed, she had to grieve her failure. Then she was able to return to her goal refreshed and renewed, capable of lovingly trying again without slipping into "punch, counter-punch." She simply persisted in trying to achieve her goal—a clean bedroom set in order by a daughter whom she wanted to teach how to be more responsible about her possessions.

This is the true power that comes from living fully in the present. You are in charge of you. You are capable of persisting in trying to get what you want dozens and even hundreds of times in a row. All you have to be able to do each and every time is to grieve your losses, your setbacks, and your crushing defeats. This requires you to develop a deep capacity to *feel* your feelings, without fearing that the intensity of your feelings will overwhelm you, crush you, or unleash terrifying forces of rage from within you. When you have that kind of self-power, you are the master over you. No outside forces can make you say or do anything that you will regret. Everything becomes a choice, and you are the chooser, the decision-maker. In the present, nothing you do is unintentional. Your actions are a conscious choice.

Your feelings are a powerful barrier to unleashing the power within you to be your most excellent self. The way your feelings get in the way is by the natural instinct each of us has to do one of two things with our feelings—bury them, or blame them. When we *bury* our feelings, we are denying how we really feel. We are maintaining our façade as a tough guy, a "super-woman," or an otherwise indestructible person. When we *blame* our feelings on someone, we also cannot grieve our losses. In a different way, we are also not acknowledging our own feelings when we are preoccupied with thoughts that say, "It's not my fault. He or she did it to me. They had no right. I'm mad at them. I'll sure as hell never forgive them." When we bury or blame, we are not taking ownership of our feelings. We are either unaware of our feelings, or they are "out there" as the fault of that other person or situation that fell upon us.

In order to grieve our losses, we must *own* our feelings, regardless of what happened, who did it, or why it happened. My nine-year-old stepdaughter Caroline gave me a good example of this one school morning. She was frantically looking for a missing running shoe. The bus was about to arrive, and she needed her running shoes for gym class that day. After searching high and low without success, she stopped dead in her tracks and began crying openly and freely. She was overcome with grief that she couldn't find the shoe that she was certain she had seen just minutes earlier. Suddenly the bus arrived. I gave her a hug, as she quickly grabbed another pair of shoes, saying laconically, "I guess I just won't have gym class today." By the time I walked her out to the waiting bus, she was smiling happily, the lost shoe now forgotten. What a beautiful example she gave of how to manage one's emotions in a crisis. She did her best, hit a wall, grieved her loss deeply, and accepted her new reality, all in less than two minutes. She never blamed herself or anyone else. She just cried that her shoe was nowhere to be found and that she would therefore not be able to participate in gym class.

We all have the power within us to do what Caroline did. When we fail in our love relationships, falter at work, upset a friend, lose a loved one to a death, or even make a bad putt, we have it within us to grieve that loss fully and completely. When we do, we heal ourselves so that we can return to the present without resentment or fear, clear-minded about what we want and confident in what's now important for us. Our confidence comes in knowing that we will handle our defeats and give ourselves the time and space we need to heal our wounds. Then we become free to see each moment as a fresh moment, without making assumptions or leaping to conclusions that just because this moment looks a lot like the many previous times that we were hurt, the same thing will happen this time. In this moment, it might happen differently. We might get what we want, and if we don't, we know that we will grieve that loss fully and completely.

A COILED SPRING

Your feelings help you to notice when things are off-track. If you understand yourself well enough, your feelings can be your guide in showing you how your past is surfacing to influence what's important now for you in this new situation. One of the areas in which you can best discover the power of feeling your feelings is in noticing how good your memory is. Have you ever observed that your memory was clearest in situations in which you felt emotionally centered? I can remember my first trip across Europe nearly twenty years ago in amazing detail. I felt excited, content, and extremely present for those three weeks. I can recall the towns, the people, the food, and the emotional highs, such as the times I was singing boisterously while riding in the train with my best friend Rob. My mind rarely thought about home. Warm childhood memories are also like that. Some of us can recall the sights, sounds, and smells of the family cottage, the fall fair, or the lazy days of summer with remarkable clarity. Even if an experience was negative, we might have a clear memory of it. As long as we feel emotionally safe, we can be present with all of our mind, body, heart, and soul. The result is that we are able to remember those moments with amazing clarity.

In order to fully tap into the joy and the power of living in the present, we must learn how to give ourselves that same feeling of emotional safety when the going appears to be rougher than we think we can handle. In those moments, we must tame our emotions so that they serve us rather than overrule us in response to attacks, rejection, or abandonment in our lives. Imagine how powerful you would be if you felt confident and secure even if your spouse were icily angry with you, your boss were menacingly threatening, or your children were unexpectedly in danger of being harmed. In each of those moments, you would be a much more effective person, capable of reacting with speed and certainty in your choice of words and deeds.

What happens for many of us instead is that we numb out emotionally in those high-pressure moments. You can tell if this has been happening to you by whether or not you are able to remember those moments very clearly. If you can't, the odds are that your feelings were partially numbed out, meaning that not all of you was present in that moment. You cannot remember something if you were not there to hear it, see it, and feel it. I have heard rape victims describe this as their experience during their rape. They felt that they were not even in their bodies. Rather, they were floating surreally above themselves, looking down at themselves as if they and their body were no longer a part of each other. This numbing out helped them to survive their traumatic and dangerous situation.

That's why we numb out. We are not safe and we know it. These are the times that can be virtually blank in our memories. I remember noticing that, whenever I had a fight with my first girlfriend, I had trouble remembering what either of us had said just moments earlier. In that same vein, many of us can meet someone new and forget their name within seconds of hearing it. For some reason, we feel a bit uptight and tense, and our mind doesn't really hear the person's name as our brain flits about nervously, self-consciously wondering if we are dressed well enough, or preoccupied with some other concern. These are examples of times when we feel emotionally unsafe. We disconnect from our emotional self, thus limiting our abilities and our potential for excellence.

Paradoxically, when our emotions are *too* intense, part of our brain also shuts down, thereby limiting our potential.

Usually, it is our capacity to think clearly that is compromised. To return to my story about Caroline's running shoe, after the bus had left, I went back into the house and immediately spotted her other shoe, sitting large as life on the cluttered kitchen countertop. I couldn't help but smile to myself. Her emotional breakdown had actually blocked her from seeing the shoe that was sitting right in front of her. Her emotions had prevented her from being as good as she wanted to be.

We often cause this reduction in our competency by undermining the legitimacy of how we feel. We judge our feelings and have critical thoughts about them. "I can't believe that I feel so nervous about making this speech!" I was often critical of myself when I forgot something or made a mistake while doing a task. I expected myself to be perfect, and when I fell short of the mark, my true emotions, once unleashed, showed my instinctive desire to lash out at myself or at someone upon whom I could pin the blame. We are undermining ourselves in these moments, making it unsafe *within ourselves*, to be fully present.

The secret to unleashing the power of your emotional self lies in the fact that your feelings must be *available* to you, yet they must also not overwhelm you. When you can achieve this state of presence, your emotions become an invaluable tool that will help you feel safe and secure, confident and ready to do what's important now for you. They will alert you to danger and opportunity, guide you as to what is causing your feeling and help you to act in a way that accelerates your success, rather than hindering it.

You must develop a good understanding of how your emotions are serving you in a given moment if you are to master your feelings. Many of us tend to be either under-emotional (burying) or over-emotional (blaming), though we are capable of being either at any given point in time. When you are being under-emotional, you are applying a lesson that you probably learned early on the road of life: your feelings can be dangerous and are not to be trusted. You might impulsively say or do something that could result in unpleasant consequences for you.

I experienced an example of this when I was twelve years old. I was swimming with a friend at a public swim area that was really just a large, muddy pond. Suddenly, I felt the need to defecate. My friend encouraged me to just go in the water. "No one will see it," he urged in a "how-can-anything-go-wrong?" kind of voice. Without another thought, I did it. A moment later, up popped a floating brown log. Other kids noticed it right away, while I slipped away as unobtrusively as I could, beaming-red with embarrassment. A lifeguard came over shortly afterwards, his face scowled in disgust as he removed my log with a five-gallon pail. Experiences like this one teach us to not only distrust other people, but also to distrust our feelings, which, in my case, were telling me to just unload my problem and thereby avoid the long walk to the outhouse. Once the crisis hit, I avoided my feelings by burying them. I put on a brave face, while my friend laughed in mocking delight at my stupidity. I tried to pretend that I was not hurting when, in fact, I felt crushed and humiliated. By burying my feelings, I put up a wall to prevent myself from doing such foolish, impulsive actions again.

Your challenge is the opposite when you are feeling over-emotional. Your emotions are a source of power, not embarrassing failure. When you hit a roadblock, you might fume and bluster, or sob and blither. The result is that other people will often respond to your feelings by *giving* you what you want. When I was twenty, I had an experience that taught me this truth. I was in my first supervisory job as the site foreman and forklift driver for a sod company. I had a thirty-two year old man working in my crew, who kept wanting to give me free "advice" about how I should be doing my job. One day, I had enough. I blew up at him, cursed him with a blue streak, and demanded that he get back to work or get the hell out of there! To my amazement, he quietly walked off, returned to his job, and treated me with a lot more respect after that. My explosive anger was nicely rewarded. He "made" me angry, and I threw the anger back in his face, with a successful result for me.

These kind of experiences teach us that blaming others "motivates" other people to do what we want. When we snap at our workers, they speed up their efforts. When we clam up in anger at our spouse, they give in to what we want. When we break down and cry, people pay attention to us and try to fix our hurt feelings by giving us what we want.

In contrast, when we are fully present our feelings are in balance. We do not shrink away from them, but we do not explode, either. My therapist, André, often spoke of this ideal state as being like a large coil—quietly ready to spring into action whenever something significant bumps into it. Our ideal emotional state is one in which we are not using our emotions to make anyone feel guilty, or to manipulate or bulldoze anyone, yet we are also *connected* to our emotions so that we notice the pings and twangs that alert us to danger. In this coiled state, we adapt and adjust in the moment, avoiding embarrassing or harmful actions while making wise and assertive choices.

To get to this extraordinary place, we must open a dangerous doorway, the doorway to *Feel Our Feelings*. This is a frightening doorway because we must face a deep fear based on two beliefs: the belief that our emotions are so powerful that they are uncontrollable, and the belief that our emotions are actually powerless. Our memory of past events—those times when other people's responses to us confirmed these two beliefs as reality—is what blocks us from opening this doorway. When other people reacted to our emotional selves by humiliating or rejecting us, they were unwittingly teaching us that our emotions have the power to make us very tiny. When they cowered and gave in to our emotional outbursts, they taught us that our feelings can make us very huge. Neither is true. All that happened was that we either triggered a belief in the other person, or we didn't. If we didn't, then perhaps they laughed at us, and we felt how powerless our emotions were. If we did trigger them, then we felt the power that our emotions could bring to change the present moment and make it what we want it to be.

If you want to live in the present, you must dare to shatter these two delusions. You must discover that just because you are showering your unhappiness onto other people, this doesn't mean that anyone "should" do something about how you feel. By the same token, just because you are burying your feelings and being logical about what you want, this also does not mean that anyone "should" give you what you want. Breaking these two delusions can be a devastating experience. You are learning that your emotions, or the lack thereof, cannot force others to meet your needs, which can leave you feeling quite powerless for a time.

As you do when you go through every other doorway, you will uncover a significant benefit for yourself. If you cannot make others do what you want using your emotions, neither can they do it to you. You become free to be true to what's right for you, even if someone who matters to you is feeling sullen, angry, annoyed, or sad because you are "making" them feel that way. Instead of shutting down or lashing out at them in the face of their emotional blaming towards you, you can remain present and centered, capable of reaching out to them with compassion and wisdom. You will be able to give them a quiet shoulder to lean on if that's what they need, or a kind word of support, or even some well-intentioned advice that isn't self-serving. After all, you know that their hurt feelings are not your fault, even if they want to blame you anyway. Then you become capable of being a coiled spring, having tamed your emotions. You become a powerful human being precisely because you trust yourself to handle your emotions with wisdom, giving yourself the chance to be the most excellent person you can be.

OWN YOUR FEELINGS

To live in the present is to say and do what you want based on whatever you are thinking and feeling in that moment. You are allowing your emotions to run freely. This is precisely the reason that living in the present is dangerous and even terrifying. Who knows what unspeakable, horrible words might come out of your mouth if you were to just react emotionally to whatever unpleasant events came along? Who knows how weak and pitiful you might look in the eyes of others if they knew how scared, how sad, or even how happy you really felt?

Guarding ourselves against our emotions is one of the main reasons all of us struggle to live fully in the present. Our emotions give us away. They betray us, showing our truth right in the moment. When the boss puts us down, we can speak our truth that we feel hurt, or we can flee by resentfully suppressing those feelings and acting tough as though nothing could hurt us. We can also fight by lashing out at him or her, trying to make them feel guilty for having hurt our feelings. Either way, we are not present to our own truth. Our truth is that we *do* feel hurt. Perhaps we even feel afraid that those unkind words mean that we're not good enough, and that our career is in jeopardy. That would be our truth.

When you own your feelings, you are claiming back your power. The boss didn't make you feel sad, angry, or humiliated. YOU felt that way all by yourself, in reaction to his or her words. When you can own this, you are in charge of you. You are then able to do something for yourself in order to soothe your feelings, without relying on your boss to take back his or her words, or apologize. Neither will you feel compelled to bury your feelings, only to have them leak out resentfully to your co-workers around the water-cooler. When you own your feelings, you become capable of releasing them in a safe way. Learning how to express your feelings safely is how you will overcome your fear of your feelings, and develop your ability to authentically handle intense emotional situations with grace and with intimacy.

A powerful way to express your feelings is to separate them from the "trigger" that ignited them in the first place. The trigger is the person or the situation that you instinctively want to blame for your feelings. "You piss me off! You're late again!" When you express your feelings in this way, you can be sure of one thing - a counter-punch! After all, your expression of your feelings will feel like a punch to the other person. You are saying, in effect, "I feel hurt and it's your fault!" When you separate your feelings from the trigger, you own them. You can do this by saying, "I feel angry that you are late." Now you've separated your feelings from their action. This technique is described as "I feel x when you do y." Expressing your emotions in this way is a powerful way to avoid burying them, while not blaming them on the other person, either. Here are some examples:

"I feel angry when you refuse to let me see my son."

"I feel nervous when you kiss me like that."

"I feel happy that you remembered my birthday."

Like any new behaviour, it will feel a bit mechanical at first. I found that I had to think consciously of it, as if it were a "rule." I usually use it when I feel myself hesitating to be authentic. That's a sign that I know I am not feeling safe. Then I pull out the, "I feel x when you do y" technique, gather up my courage, and speak up.

This doesn't guarantee that the other person won't try to "emotionally" punch you anyway. They may still take personally the fact that you are feeling that way, even if you didn't accuse them of that. If someone is late and you say, "I feel angry that you are late," they may retort, "Hey, don't get mad at me! The traffic was awful. Besides, you're often late, too, and I don't get mad at you!" For most of us, our emotional response mechanisms are automatic, and in this example, it is likely that the other person would not even notice that you did not accuse them by saying you were "mad at them." The beauty of this technique is that you have put yourself in a position in which you won't feel compelled to react defensively to their "punch." You can respond by saying, "I didn't say I was mad at you. I only said that I feel angry when you are late." If they are wise, they will simply empathise with your angry feelings. However, most people will tend to want to "fix" your angry feelings. They will try in some way to convince you that you *shouldn't* feel angry. If you get drawn into that kind of debate, you have given away your power as you try to convince them that your feelings are indeed justified. At that moment, you are deciding that what's important now is to link your sense of self-worth to whether they affirm or deny your angry feelings. When you are fully present, what matters is that *you* acknowledged your own feelings in a safe way. You didn't bury them, and you didn't blame the other person. You were authentic and true to yourself, which means that you did not abandon yourself by choosing to protect the other person from your truth, or to protect yourself from their potential reaction to your truth.

There are two keys to the effectiveness of this way of self-disclosing your feelings. One is in the accuracy with which you specify the other person's behaviour. If you are very accurate, repeating precisely the words they said or the action they did, you give them no reason to be defensive. They can hardly deny a specific behaviour that they have displayed. You enter the danger zone when you are vague, add an untrue twist, or label their behaviour. For example, when you say "I feel angry that you are late," you are still being vague. A more specific disclosure would be, "I feel angry that you are arriving home at seven-thirty, when you said that you would be home by six o'clock." Now the focus is more sharply on how you feel, not on what they did. You have created an environment in which it will feel safer for them to *acknowledge* how you feel, rather than to *debate* what they did. "I'm sorry that you feel angry. How can I make it up to you?" Isn't that the dream response we all want? The unpleasant alternative is that the other person will get into an argument about whether he or she really said "six o'clock," or whether you perhaps misunderstood or misheard what they actually said. The more present you were in the first place, the more likely it is that you will accurately remember what each of you said and did.

The second key to making "I feel x when you feel y" work for you is to use "pure feeling" words to describe how you feel. There are five pure feelings: anger, sadness, fear, joy, and lust. Other "feeling words," such as irritated, annoyed, frustrated, hateful, excited, bored, anxious, and so on, are "hybrid" feelings—"pure" feelings with a twist. For example, I feel annoyed really means, "I feel *mildly* angry." I feel anxious really means, "I feel *a little bit* afraid." The first advantage of using these five feelings is that they give you a short list with which to check in to your self. "Which of the five feelings am I having?" is very simple compared to trying to determine whether your anger is irritation, annoyance, or frustration. The second advantage of using pure feelings is that you have to own the feeling totally. When you use "hybrid feeling" words, you are taking the edge off your feelings, as in, "I am not really angry, I'm just a *little bit* angry." The danger is that when someone reacts defensively, you will abandon yourself by saying, "Okay, maybe I'm not really irritated after all. Maybe I was wrong and I really shouldn't be feeling that way at all." Generally, I find that it doesn't take much of a nudge to avoid owning your feelings and to begin burying them or blaming them on others.

PROTECTOR AND INNER CHILD

You must dare to feel your feelings in the moment in which they are actually happening if you want to achieve the personal excellence that comes from living in the present. That is the reason that you are taking down all your walls, so that you will be instantly connected to your emotional self, along with your physical, mental, and spiritual self. I want to explain how a person can go about intentionally cultivating that connection, so that you can tap into your emotional self in the moment. This is so important because it often happens that we have a feeling but don't really know where it came from or what caused it. We just suddenly notice that we are feeling unexpectedly sad, or angry, or nervous. These feelings are like signal lights, telling us that we need to do something for ourselves *right now*, in order to feel safe again.

When you learn how to read your emotional signals and respond appropriately, you will dramatically improve your self-trust that you can count on yourself to do what's important for you in the present moment.

The way that you can do this is by noticing the voices that are going on inside your head. When you are debating a decision, you will no doubt notice that there is often more than one voice going on in your mind. One voice is urging you to "Go for it!," while another voice is saying, "Be careful! You might get burned if you do this." Cartoons often depict these two voices as an angel on one shoulder and the devil on the other shoulder. Taking notice of the fact that you are having such a conversation is the start to connecting to your emotions, and then dealing with them effectively.

As I began to remove my walls of self-protection, I became aware that one of my inner voices actually filtered my emotional impulses and made "rational" decisions on what I would actually do, regardless of what I was feeling. I called this voice "Protector." Protector is the rational voice that weighs your decisions, considers your options, and stops you from acting in a dangerous or unsafe way. At first I thought this voice was just my normal and total self. As I became conscious of this voice, I recognized a second voice. This second voice was wanting something. André later described this voice as my "Inner Child." Our Inner Child is the irrational voice that is like a three-year-old, driven purely by emotion. Protector, on the other hand, is the rational adult voice that makes all the decisions. "Protector is like a computer," André said to me, "devoid of emotion and purely processing what he thinks is best for you." Well, I noticed that Protector liked pointing out mostly what was bad about what my Inner Child was wanting. Protector always seemed to be the dominant voice in my mental conversations. For example:

Inner Child: It's such a nice day. I feel like going golfing with Bill.

Protector: Oh, but I have so much work to do!

Inner Child: Yeah, but I've worked really hard this week.

Protector: If I don't get that report done, I'm toast! My client will be royally ticked off with me.

Whenever I got to this point in my mental conversations, I would notice the adrenaline begin to surge in my body at the prospect of Jerry's anger. Then I would begin to rationalize, using role-play-thinking.

Inner Child: What can I tell him so that he'll be okay? I did promise him I'd have it done by today… But I really want to go golfing! Maybe I'll tell him I had an emergency with another client.

Protector: He's not going to like hearing that some other client got priority over him! I've got to get this report done! (Sinking feeling in pit of stomach).

Of course, I might go through various versions of this for several minutes. Usually, I would decide to do the "right thing." I would over-ride my Inner Child while feeling resentful about doing so. However, the less numbed out I became, the more powerful the resentment and the urgings of my Inner Child became. Removing my walls was having the effect of bringing my Inner Child's voice back to life, with energy and passion that was both wonderful and frightening at the same time.

When we steamroll our Inner Child, we are burying our emotions. Our Protector voice is acting like a drill sergeant, taking control of our Inner Child in spite of how we are feeling. The only way we can do this and get away with it is by burying those feelings, or by blaming somebody else in order to justify what our drill sergeant Protector is demanding that we do. In the above example, if I did go golfing, I might justify it by blaming my client, saying, "Screw Jerry. He's given me such a hard time on this project. He'll just have to like it or lump it that I'm a day late." I've avoided my true feelings of anxiety about being a day late by blaming Jerry as a person who is hard to work with and deserves to be treated badly by me.

On the other hand, if I didn't go golfing even though I really wanted to, I am burying my true feelings, saying to myself, "Don't be such a lazy bum. You can't play all the time. You've got to get some work done first!" These are beliefs that Protector often relies on to justify whatever decision you ultimately make.

One of the dangers of becoming conscious of your inner voices is that you may project them onto someone else. When I separated from my wife, I initially perceived Protector to be the sound of my ex-wife's voice. I felt enraged as I discovered this! At that time, I was still in a heavy "blame-my-wife" mode. I thought to myself, "She is so controlling that she has actually ingrained herself into my psyche! She is telling me I can't do things, even before I ever say a word to her! No wonder I feel so controlled!" However, with André's help, I began to see what is now patently obvious. Protector was my own voice. Protector took on the appearance of my ex-wife's voice because her approval of my actions had become so important to me. In slowing down my mind, I could see that I was having entire conversations in my mind with her. In my inner "role-play-thinking," she was rejecting my wants, giving all of her reasons. As a result, I would begin to feel angry and frustrated with her response, feeling controlled by her. With constant self-awareness, I realized that I would get angry with her before she had even heard a word from me about the subject. How unfair for both of us! I was the one denying myself. I was my own worst critic. I decided that I wanted to eject this demon from my mind. André slowed me down. "You cannot banish that which is a part of you," he said. "Instead, embrace the voice. Accept the voice. Protector is serving you. Protector can be helpful." His words stopped me in my tracks. I could see the sense in what he was saying. It was true that I rarely allowed my emotions to be a factor in my decisions. However, I could see that always making decisions based on only my emotions could also be unhealthy.

André wanted me to focus on the other voice in the conversation. I began to see a picture form in my mind. I could see a little boy. The little boy was curled up in fetus form. He was perhaps four years old. He looked limp but not lifeless. The little boy looked like me when I was a boy. I recalled my first dialogue at The Option Institute, when I first discovered that I was so afraid of my feelings. That first time, my little boy appeared to me as if in a cage, all locked up. He was no longer in a cage. He was exposed and vulnerable.

André invited me to explore my Inner Child. "What is he feeling?"

"He feels afraid," I responded.

"What is he afraid of?"

"That he'll be angry, lash out."

"How do you feel about letting him do that?"

"Scared. I don't know what I might do. I might do something really crazy. I don't trust myself."

André noticed that my voice became very even, very unemotional. "What is happening?" he asked. "Who is talking now?"

"I don't know," I mumbled. He let me think about it. "Protector, I guess."

Then he invited me to act out the two voices. He pulled up another chair. "Switch from chair to chair, as you switch voices. Protector will sit here. Your Inner Child will sit there."

I tried this. First in Protector's chair. Then to my Inner Child's chair. I hated to move over there. I felt very uncomfortable. My stomach churned. I felt tight as a drum. A terrible picture formed in my mind. I was enraged. I was beating up the little boy. I wanted to hurt that little boy so badly. I could see myself flailing away in anger, a big adult beating up a little boy. The little boy was cowering in fear, curled up yet curiously quiet, simply absorbing the beating.

I escaped fast. André could see it immediately. My voice died out. My body language closed up. I did not want to go there. "My God," I thought, "What have I uncovered? Why do I want to beat myself up so badly? I must really think I am an awful and unlovable person."

Eventually, I came to see that that was exactly what I believed. I wasn't just a bad person. I was terrible and evil. I could see that many key events in my life had taught me that I was an unlovable person. Bad to the core. It probably started when I was a very young child. My father being very angry with me and beating me, albeit infrequently, "when I deserved it." My friends rejecting me cruelly when I was thirteen, in response to my crying and temper tantrums. My first wife regularly reminding me that I was forgetful, thoughtless, self-centered, and incapable of being a good father. These had all blended together in my mind. They were all correct as far as I was concerned. I was all of those things. I was a bad person to the core.

André encouraged me to let my feelings out. "Express the anger," he said, "but do it safely. You need to run to the top of the mountain, pull out your sword, and wave it in the sun. Don't use the sword, just own it and express it." He suggested that I buy a boxing bag and simply punch it whenever I felt angry. I took his advice. I bought a huge punching bag. What a release! I could feel enormous amounts of negative energy pouring out of my body. Whether you punch a bag, the back of a chair, or a pillow, you will find it helpful to connect to the cause of your anger when you learn how to express it safely first. Punching a boxing bag does not cure the source of your feelings. What it does do is allow the emotion to escape so that you can see more clearly what you need to do for yourself in order to solve the underlying issue. If you don't go to the point of taking action, you will be punching pillows for a long time, every time this trigger gets touched by some event in your life.

André called the battle between Protector and Inner Child one that is between Top Dog and Under Dog. He said that while Top Dog might get his way most of the time, sooner or later, Under Dog will have his way, too. You have to learn how to hear and respect both of these voices if you are going to feel at peace within yourself. Making peace with these two voices means becoming conscious of them. You must want to feel your feelings right when an event is occurring. You must no longer want to "realize" ten minutes, ten hours, or even ten years after the fact that you felt angry or afraid or frustrated or whatever! This has to be a top priority. If you don't do this, sooner or later, Under Dog will surface whether you like it or not. He or she surfaces in the form of an illness. Your body and your Inner Child are intertwined to the point where they are really one and the same. When you treat your body well, you are loving your Inner Child. By the same token, when you treat your Inner Child well, you are loving your body. This explains for me why my own physical health has improved so much. My *permafrost* has melted and my body has healed itself, while maintaining my weight and strength in good balance, all without any extra effort on my part.

The best way that I know of to notice how safe your inner

child feels is during sex. When I feel unsafe, I notice that I am not fully present. Rather than seeing my body from my eyes' perspective (that is, unable to see my face, head and back), I am seeing my entire self as if I were watching myself on a movie screen. I especially notice this during masturbation. If my fantasy feels unsafe, I see myself as if I were watching myself in a fantasy scene in a movie. When I change my fantasy scene to one in which I am with someone with whom I feel safe, I am suddenly in the movie itself, and my sexual arousal sparks noticeably. Another way that my mind will wander during sex is when I suddenly start thinking about tasks that need to be done. For reasons like not trusting myself about future tasks aching to be done (based on past failures of mine), Protector is intervening and my Inner Child begins to numb out. By contrast, when I feel safe during sex, Protector fades away while my Inner Child is fully present in a fun, playful and energetic way.

If you want to take a huge step towards the excellence that comes from living in the present, you must embrace your Inner Child. Regularly check in with what is happening to your Inner Child. Visualize what he or she looks like in this moment. That vision will tell you in an instant whether you are feeling sad, mad, glad, joyous, or lustful. If you cannot connect to one of these five pure feelings, then you are probably numbed out. Feeling your feelings in this moment is not safe for you. What's important now for you is to escape. As time goes by and you learn how to release your emotions safely, you will see your mental picture change as your Inner Child comes out regularly. In those moments, you will begin to experience joy and love in ways that you didn't know were even possible.

Up to this point, our focus was mostly on how we abandon our Inner Child by *burying* our feelings. When we *blame* our feelings on others, we are actually doing the opposite of this. Our Inner Child feels exposed to danger, and he or she feels frightened. So we lash out, trying to make the danger go away. When we blame others, we are trying to change them in some way, including pushing them away so that we won't feel we are in danger. In reality, the danger is from within ourselves. Our Protector voice is not doing the job. Rather than being too dominant, Protector is not strong enough. For a lot of reasons that are rooted in our child-hood, we did not learn how to assert ourselves adequately. The result is that we rely on our emotions to protect us, rather than also leaning on our mental skills that are a part of that rational, computer-like voice known as Protector, Inner Adult, or Inner Critic.

Unlike people who are intensely logical, over-emotional people must learn how to tap into their intellectual strengths in moments of crisis. The only reason over-emo-tional people are over-emotional is that they feel unsafe and unprotected. The remedy for this is the same that would be appropriate for people who are under-emotional. They must *own* their feelings. When you claim your feelings, you are reassuring your Inner Child that he or she has been heard. When your Inner Child feels heard, your emotions will sub-side, allowing your logical faculties to more competently assess what you should do. When you are truly present, you also invite your Inner Knowing to come into your aware-ness, guiding you as to what's important now for you.

LISTENING IN THE PRESENT

Once you connect to your feelings and truly own them as yours, then you must find ways to release them safely. Otherwise, the danger is that you may get stuck where you are. You will have developed a great deal of courage to be authentic, risk disapproval, believe that others' feelings are not about you, and be willing to let go of your attachment to various outcomes that might have previously motivated you to bury your feelings within yourself. Now your Protector voice is less able to keep those feelings within. The danger for you is that you will become a bundle of constant emotions.

You will notice this mostly in day-to-day situations. When you get stuck in a long lineup at the grocery store, you will notice just how annoyed you feel because you expected to be in and out of the store in ten minutes. You will notice how you feel frustrated on a cold day when the gas pump is so slow to fill up your car. You will truly feel your irritation that the person you wanted to reach is unavailable and doesn't appear to be making an effort to return your calls.

Let's say that you have an appointment with someone and they show up an hour late, not having called you or done anything to forewarn you. Let's further say that this is the umpteenth time that this has happened with this person. Perhaps you used to be able to bottle up those feelings once the person arrived, paste an inauthentic smile on your face, and reassure them that you really didn't mind their tardiness, and furthermore, that you were able to figure out how to achieve world peace while you were waiting. However, that was before you became so present. Now with your walls down, you feel annoyed and much less capable of hiding your feelings. Your Inner Child starts having angry thoughts: "That jerk. He's always late. It really bugs me when he does this to me! He is so inconsiderate of me and my time! Do I ever do that to him? Never!" Then your mind might go off in a variety of directions, all with thoughts of "teaching him a lesson" and "doing the same to him next time and see how he likes it." Your Inner Child is out in full force, ready to have a temper tantrum and let the other person have it. Your feelings are in high gear, and you are now in danger of saying or doing something you may regret later.

However, if you look at this a little deeper, you will find that part of your anger is directed at yourself. If you connect to this level of self-awareness, you might then ask yourself, "Why did I let myself agree to see this guy again? He is always late! You would think I would learn, but instead I keep trusting that sweet-talking liar!" We are rarely angry with someone else without being partially angry with ourselves, too, for letting ourselves get into that situation. Even if the other person seems totally to blame, like a spouse who cheated or a boss who lied, at some level, you are likely to also blame yourself. Like a real child, some part of you wants to believe that you could have somehow prevented this painful disaster if only you had been smart enough not to marry that person, not to take on that job in the first place, or not to have agreed to meet with this always-tardy person. When you are angry with yourself, your Inner Child is no longer safe. In that moment, your Inner Child is likely to disappear into a curled-up fetus position in the corner, limp and lifeless.

As you get closer to what is actually happening in your mind in the moment, you will see that your anger is in response to your own self-criticism. Your Inner Child is heaping abuse upon Protector. "Why did you do that, you idiot!" I would lash out at myself. I recalled first noticing this self-directed rage while I was in university. I forgot my briefcase at home after I had driven thirty miles back to school. I was enraged! I slammed my fist onto the console of my car and onto my steering wheel over and over again. I cursed a blue streak and screamed in a fit of anger. "How could I be so incredibly stupid?" I fumed at my own unforgivable stupidity. In these moments, your Inner Child is having a temper tantrum.

With persistence, I began to see that I did this to myself much more frequently than I realized. As I tried to control my anger, I unconsciously built a wall in order to contain the danger that I felt from my explosive rage. When you do that to yourself, you are no longer emotionally present. You will likely experience very low emotional energy. Your passion will be weak, and you may just be going through the motions in survival mode. You are working with only half of your brain—the intellectual half. You might be mentally present, but you are not emotionally present. Therefore, you are not fully present. You are not alert, confident, and capable of being your very best. This is when you may notice that your memory starts to be noticeably less effective. Your emotional self is buried, numbed out, and disconnected. You must find ways to make it "safe" for your Inner Child to emerge. That is much easier said than done. If anything, becoming aware that my Inner Child was crawling back into his cocoon right when I most needed to be emotionally present, would leave me feeling even more angry! This, of course, made it even more unsafe for me to "feel" my feelings. After hitting my head against that rock wall for a good long period of time, I realized that it was impossible to *force* myself into reconnecting to my feelings in a given moment. Instead, I had to *create* a safe environment in which my Inner Child and my feelings could naturally resurface. Otherwise, my mental capabilities were immediately dulled. We cannot think clearly when we are over-emotional. In both situations, we have to return to our emotional center, being neither too emotional, nor too numbed out.

The best way in which to bring your Inner Child back to center is to affirm your feelings using a technique that I call

"Listening in the Present." This is a four-step technique with which you are tuning into your Inner Child and resolving your feelings, right in the moment. *Listening in the Present* works because you are reassuring your Inner Child that you are not abandoning him or her. Rather, you are affirming that your feelings are real and valid. The unconscious message to yourself and to others is that you are lovable and worthy of positive attention, which leaves your Inner Child feeling safe. When you apply this simple technique to yourself, you are creating the foundation for grieving your present loss, no matter how big or small it may be. *Listening in the Present* is remarkably easy to explain and do, when you are conscious about it. Nevertheless, you will struggle to actually do it as you fight your desire to bury or blame your feelings rather than own them. This is a normal part of the struggle to live more fully in the present.

The four steps to *Listening in the Present* are captured in the acronym M.E.A.D., that is, Mirror, Empathize, Assert, and Do:

1. **Mirror**—Identify and say how you feel, capturing the words, the body language, and the tone of voice as you actually feel it. "I feel angry. I feel really, really angry! I am so PISSED OFF! *I could scream, I'm so angry!!"* This is how you confirm to your Inner Child that he or she is not alone but is being *heard* by you, by your Protector voice.

2. **Empathize**—Seek to understand and affirm your Inner Child's feelings. Say to yourself, "It's okay to feel angry. You really wanted this project to work out, and it's upsetting that Bob has changed his mind about doing it." Now you are communicating with your Inner Child that he or she is safe, even if Bob had every right to change his

mind, and even if your emotions are not fully justified or logical.

3. **Assert**—Once your emotions have calmed down, your mind will become clear to assert what you *need* to do for yourself. This is when your Protector voice can do a good job for you. "Let's not give up on it yet. Let's go back to Bob next week and find out if there is anything we can do that would encourage him to change his mind about the project." Now you are being wise, doing what's important for your Inner Child to feel safe and centered.

4. **Do**—Deliver the goods. No one feels heard, including your own Inner Child, if you don't do what you said you would do. This is a joint task of Inner Child and Protector. Protector makes the decision to do it, while Inner Child provides the emotion and the passion to make it happen freely, willingly, and without resentment. The result will be the excellence that comes when all of you is present with the task at hand, which in this case is to go and see Bob without delay.

The power of affirming your feelings through *Listening in the Present* is most clear when you look at how feelings are resolved through the eyes of a two-year-old child. Is a two-year-old logical? Not a chance. A two-year-old is an example of God's perfect creation of humankind before he or she gets "socialized." A two-year-old wants what he or she wants. When my son Jared was two, I would occasionally ask him *why* he wanted something. He always responded in the same way. "Because I want it!" He could not explain it anymore than I could satisfy him with a logical reason why he couldn't have it. He did not care that it was an hour's drive to his grandfather's house and that it was now bedtime. He wanted to go there, right now! Telling him that he couldn't go simply set off an emotional display of fireworks. He dialed up his anger. He started to cry. He crawled down onto the floor and pounded his tiny fists on the carpet, repeating over and over again that he wanted to go there. He pursued what he wanted with passion and persistence. Any parent of a determined toddler will recognize this as a familiar scene. What did Jared want? He wanted to be heard. He wanted to be validated and affirmed. I found that when I *mirrored* back to him what he was wanting and *empathized* with how he was feeling, he responded by letting go of his emotional tempest and returning to feeling centered. One example of this was in church. Jared would suddenly blurt out for the whole congregation to hear, "Daddy, I'm hungry!" I would immediately *mirror* his words back to him, saying, "You're hungry!" in a similar tone of voice to his. He would respond by repeating what he wanted, but in a much lower voice. "Yeah. I'm really hungry." Then I would *mirror* his words back to him again. "You're really hungry, aren't you?" I would say, using a softer voice. I would patiently do this as often as four or five times. Every time, he would let it go, and we would finish off the service in peace without my ever having to assert myself by saying "no," or by giving in to his emotional demands. As Jared became three and four years old, he wasn't so easily put off and would demand an answer. Then I had to apply steps three and four. I had to *assert* my position and then *do* what I asserted.

Your Inner Child is no different. No child wants to be ignored! No child wants to hear that they are not going to get what they want. And neither does the Inner Child within you and me. When we override our Inner Child's voice, we are ignoring ourselves. Most two-year-olds are convinced that they are the center of the universe. The Inner Child inside us also thinks that he or she is the center of the universe. The key to overcoming this angry little voice inside is to treat your Inner Child with respect. Mirroring and empathizing with your feelings in this present moment is how you do that. Once your feelings are validated in this way, you become emotionally capable of considering the "sensible" choices before you. This is where asserting comes in, when you are capable of doing what is the right thing for you to do in the moment, regardless of how you are actually feeling. In the end, you may still do the same thing you would have done if you had simply buried your Inner Child. The difference will be that you will feel good about the decision, rather than being resentful and potentially explosive about the issue.

By noticing your authentic thoughts in the moment, you may discover that when you are angry, you treat yourself with a remarkably harsh hand. If you have very little empathy for your Inner Child's desires and feelings, you might ask yourself, "If this were how your own child felt, is this how you would treat him or her?" The odds are that you would not. So the question becomes, "Can you give to yourself what you would give to your own child?"

Finally, be aware of jumping the gun, as you would if you tried to figure out *why* you are feeling the way you are *before* you have truly embraced the feeling. This is merely escaping the feeling. You will return to the present much quicker if you *mirror* the feeling. You may need to do this several times. I love doing this in my car. If I am very angry, I will pound my fist on my steering wheel, several times, but never hard enough to hurt myself. This probably looks a little strange to other drivers on the road. I'm okay with that because I'm doing this for me, not for them. They are entitled to think whatever they want about my behavior, as I am expressing my feelings safely, with no intent to harm anyone.

Once you have mirrored and empathized with your feelings, then you must *assert* what you want. This is much easier if you can connect back to the actual moment that triggered your emotion in the first place. Let's say you are having a busy, productive day at work, when you suddenly notice that you feel demotivated around mid-afternoon. Maybe you are a bit puzzled by this sudden drop in energy. You sit down, you mirror your feelings back to yourself (I feel lousy), and you empathize with yourself (I can understand that—I've had a huge day). Then you try to *assert* what to do. You search back in your mind for when you first felt lousy. Suddenly, you remember that it happened during your conversation with a work colleague. You felt triggered when she said, "I think Bob's project is really going to fly." You realize that that if Bob's project flies, maybe yours won't. Now you look at that possibility, grieve your potential loss, and then begin to see what's important for you to do in light of this new information. You decide that you should set up a meeting with your boss to discuss the risks associated with your project. You instantly feel much better. Then you pick up the phone, make that call to your boss, and now you are feeling centered again, since you have done what was important for you, in this present moment.

As you live more fully in the present, you will instantaneously notice these trigger events, the thoughts in your mind, and how you are feeling. You will respect that these are the signals to indicate that you are having an emotion to alert you to the fact that something is unsafe. Sometimes you will connect rather quickly. Other times you won't. If you are immediately unsuccessful, then wait. Trust that it will come back to you. It usually will if you really want it to. And when the moment does, you will then either recognize it as something that isn't serving you anymore and let it go, or you will know what's important now for you in order to remedy the situation.

When you acknowledge how you feel, you begin to heal yourself. The more you do it, the faster you will return to feeling present. The amazing part is that you don't need to do it with another person. You are talking to yourself, assuring yourself that you hear and understand your hurt feelings. You are being your own best friend. André called this developing a "benevolent parent" to support you in your times of need and to soften the blows from the critical Protector voice within that you inherited from your parents, teachers, spouse, and other mentors whose approval mattered to you along in your past life. You have to learn how to be a competent child before you can become a competent adult. A big part of that journey is to recognize the times when you are not being a competent child, and to make the effort to learn what you did not learn when you were a young child.

COMMON ESCAPES

When you remove your walls and feel your feelings, you will notice all the events that trigger you. Your feelings will get even more intense, and it won't take long before this intensity begins to hurt. Most of us are imperfect, and so you, too, will regularly fail to own your feelings in the moment. You will slip back into burying or blaming your feelings, just to ease the pain of their intensity. When you do, you may find yourself slipping into some very common forms of escape.

One day, André explained to me that men, in particular, escape from their emotions in two ways. "They go up, or they go down," he said, pointing to his temple and then to his genitals. My way was to be analytical. I was far too uptight to escape sexually. André went on to explain how we must break this deeply ingrained habit. He took a deep breath and said, "You've got to lose your mind and come to your senses." He told me that he was quoting the founder of Gestalt therapy, Fritz Perls. If André said it once to me, he said it fifty times. When we lose our minds, we are not "in our heads," thinking, analyzing, or rationalizing. We have let go of all thoughts. Without thoughts in our minds, we are able to fully connect to our emotions. We become fully present. When we are "in our heads," we tend to get analytical, or to tell stories. "I wonder why I am having that feeling?" is a way to start the analysis and to kill the feeling all in the same moment. Escaping by telling stories usually begins with, "I remember feeling this way once when ..." This will usually send you off onto a completely new tangent, causing you to escape your present feeling completely!

Your body also gives away how you might be trying to escape from your feelings. If André and I got close to a subject that stirred my feelings, he would watch my body language and later give me feedback. He observed that I would close up physically. I would cross my legs. I would cross my arms. My breathing would become very shallow and my shoulders would become hunched up. My voice would become quiet and monotone, with little energy. These were all signs that I was numbing out because I was getting too close to really feeling my feelings in that very moment.

Another way to escape is to begin to laugh. This happened to me regularly, and André would say to me, "You are telling me about a serious event that happened to you, yet you are laughing. What is so funny about this? It sounds rather tragic to me!" I would respond rather sheepishly, "I know it's not funny. I have no idea why I want to laugh. It just happens. I remember that once in Grade 3, my teacher was giving me heck, and I burst out laughing right in her face. She turned five shades of red. I think she wanted to throttle me." Ah-h. Another scary moment avoided, as I escaped André's question with another story. But he wasn't so easily diverted, I am grateful to say.

Addictions are another major way in which we bury our feelings. Addictions numb our pain. We give ourselves a temporary boost, a calm feeling that makes us feel better, albeit short-lived. When we drink alcohol or get high on dope, we are numbing our pain. When we smoke a cigarette or take drugs, we are numbing our pain. When we compulsively over-gamble, over-work, over-eat, over-sex, over-shop or get overly-busy, we are escaping from the pain that pulses within us, aching to be healed if only we would let ourselves completely *feel* that pain. But to allow ourselves to feel that level of pain is to risk crossing this dangerous doorway of feeling our feelings. So we pour on our addictive liniments, basking in the temporary relief they give us.

My favorite addictive escape was smoking. My struggle to overcome this drug-based way of numbing out proved to be a powerful means of healing my fear of my emotions. I want to share my experience in overcoming this addiction, so that you might appreciate how your own addictions might be serving you, and how you can overcome them. I began smoking when I was fourteen. I quit when I was twenty. Over the next twenty years, I started and quit smoking six more times, never smoking for more than a few months at a time. After hating myself for starting the fifth time, I began to reframe my beliefs about my smoking. Instead of beating myself up while reminding myself of the fifty reasons I should not be smoking, I decided that my addiction was serving me. Some part of me wanted to smoke. No outside force like "when I have a drink," or "when I'm at a party" was making me do it. I no longer saw myself as "needing" a smoke—I was *choosing* to smoke. I accepted that there must be a positive reason that smoking was what was important now for me, or else why would I do it?

The first thing that I noticed when I reframed my beliefs in this way was that I felt much more at peace about my addiction. My ferocious battle between my Inner Child (I want a smoke!) and my Inner Adult/Protector voice (don't do it—okay, go ahead…) eased considerably. The second thing I noticed was that I became capable of actually looking at the beast called "my addiction to nicotine." Prior to that, I felt reluctant to look at it because I was too afraid of the beating that I would inevitably give myself for being so "weak" and "stupid." When I looked more closely at my addiction, I began to notice the pattern of events that triggered my desire to smoke. My pattern was that whenever my emotions were very intense, I felt a powerful urge to smoke. Oddly enough, it wasn't just when I felt unbearably depressed, it was also when I felt incredibly joyous, as I did on my first trip to Europe with my friend Rob. If you talk to smokers, most of them will tell you that smoking soothes them and calms their nerves. This is another way of saying that it numbs their emotional pain. Smoking after sex now made some sense to me for the first time. We are very emotionally vulnerable during sex. After sex, we are intensely aware of our emotional vulnerability. In the face of this unconscious awareness of our "unsafeness," some of us feel motivated to numb out so that our true emotions don't emerge. We light up a smoke and suddenly we feel better. In truth, we feel better because we feel *less*.

What triggers you to eat too much, drink too much, gamble too much, work too much, or pursue phone sex, strippers, and prostitutes? Is it the calming effects that accompany such activities? Oddly enough, feeling intense positive emotions can feel just as dangerous to us as feeling intense negative emotions. When we were kids, our over-enthusiasm often led our parents and teachers to crack down on us, telling us to quiet down, don't disturb daddy or the class, and stop being so much trouble! We learned to *contain* the intensity of our emotions, even when those emotions were all about passionate fun.

Becoming aware of what triggers you to escape your emotions will help you to rise above whatever addictions you may have. How does this help you overcome them? By accepting them. When you can accept *how* your addiction is serving you, you can begin to stop beating yourself up. Instead, you can find a voice of tolerance, patience, and support for yourself. You can visualize your Inner Child and hug him or her, rather than drowning your Inner Child's voice with alcohol, nicotine, drugs, or busy-aholism.

Addictions are a way to abandon ourselves. We are denying our true feelings by burying them so that we don't feel them. When you accept that doing your addictive behavior is what's important now for you, you begin to paradoxically open the door to healing the underlying cause of your addiction. You must dare to embrace your addiction. You must accept that you love to overeat and you may overeat and stay overweight for the rest of your life. You must accept that your smoking is something that serves you and that as long as it does, you may smoke for the rest of your life. You must stop the battle between your Inner Child and your Inner Critic/Protector voice by validating your feelings when you give in to your addiction. When you do that, you are loving yourself. You are breaking the self-fulfilling prophecy cycle that says, "I'm so afraid that I'll smoke/drink/eat/gamble again, that I might as well just do it, so I can stop feeling anxious and afraid that I might do it."

Instead, you become open to understanding how the addiction is serving you and perhaps finding other ways to meet that underlying need.

As I embraced this philosophy, I began to look at my cigarette from time to time right before I inhaled it, and to say to myself, "I have a choice right now. I could butt this out, or I could take another drag. I choose to take a drag." I felt my shame about my "weakness" begin to go away. I stopped any efforts I previously made to hide my smoking. I became authentic about it. I rose above my fear that if I accepted my addiction, it would be as if I were giving myself permission to smoke. I *was* giving myself that permission. One day, my smoking ended in a most unexpected way, and I have not smoked since. I believe that when I embraced the "paradoxical intention" of letting go of my desire to not smoke, accepting myself as someone who smoked from time to time, I laid the groundwork for letting go of my addiction. The secret to success was that I deeply accepted my addiction, without any expectation of an outcome that somehow this would lead me to quitting. I accepted that I might never quit. Then I became able to quit.

Our addictions are also a way of keeping up our façade as being "successful" and "in control," when in fact we feel inadequate and unlovable. In the men's group I attended, a new man joined our group who was seriously addicted to hard drugs, alcohol, and cigarettes. He was a handsome, gentle man in his late forties, who won our hearts. Every week, he went to the neighboring bar to fuel up his courage with at least two stiff drinks, in order to come to the group. If he made it, he sat pleasantly and did what he could to avoid participating. He did not want to be discovered. If the group's attention turned towards him and his issues, he found brilliant ways in which to avoid the pain of looking at his issues, dancing around them and answering questions with questions to repel our desire to be "helpful." He admitted that he had been sexually assaulted by a man when he was just ten years old. He acknowledged how he felt that the assault was his own fault, even though he was just an innocent boy at the time. He mourned the break-up of his first marriage due to his addictive habits. He knew that his current marriage was on the rocks for the same reason. He was also in danger of losing his job. Nothing we could say or do seemed to help. The addictions that soothed his inner pain with each pill, each snort, and each drink were slowly crushing him. Within a year, he quit the group. He did not want to feel his feelings or remove his walls. The doorway to feeling the intensity of his rage and his self-hatred was just too scary for him. He preferred to numb out every day with his bottle and his drugs. He was doing what was important now for him—escaping.

Such is the allure of the instant gratification that comes from addictive behaviors. The drinker relies on the mellow numbing out that each drink feeds into the bloodstream, as does the dope-smoker. The gambler gets the high of the occasional win, along with the fantasy-thinking that today will be the day that he'll really win big. The work-aholic gets a high from each achievement, though she is left aching for a bigger, better achievement as the previous high slips quickly into the past. Any compulsive, obsessive behavior reflects a desire to escape our inner pains in order to alter our present reality, making us feel better than we really feel. We cannot feel our feelings as long as we keep finding ways to escape from them. When we succumb to an addiction, we are letting ourselves get out of balance. We are sacrificing our physical bodies, our emotional health, and our mental peace of mind in order to pursue our temporary "fix." We must learn how to relieve our pain if we are to dare to live fully in the present, at peace with who we are, and capable of being the best we can be.

In the end, the only one who undermines your feelings is you yourself. Your inner critic, Protector, may be as tough as nails on your Inner Child. You may expect yourself to be perfect and to make no mistakes. Being authentic, vulnerable, and risking the loss of approval from others are frightening prospects. When you can give yourself support and empathy for whatever your words and deeds are, you give yourself the chance to fully feel your feelings. You are also helping yourself to make wise decisions that are good for you, and good for others, even if they don't agree with you.

We can only fully experience our feelings when we are present. Our emotions are God's gift to us, alerting us to danger and loss. Emotions link us to the beliefs that we have built up over the years, the rules which we have learned on the road of life to protect ourselves and be the best we can be based on what we have experienced thus far in life. Feelings are also the guideposts that allow us to bring our past beliefs into our awareness. Once these deep beliefs are in our conscious awareness, we have the opportunity to take action, either by acting on them, or by changing them. Either way, the reward is to feel present and at peace. Doing neither is to remain stuck.

When you reconnect to your emotions, "not dealing with it" becomes nearly impossible. You will feel compelled to act, though always with the awareness that you have a choice in how you deal with your feelings. Your feelings don't run you. You are in charge of you, and you make the decisions as to what's important now for you. When you do so in a way that leaves you with no regrets, and without a reason to distrust the future, then you can be confident that you will handle your future feelings effectively because you know that you have grieved and released your present feelings.

Here are some closing thoughts on *Feel Your Feelings*...

Remember...

- You must grieve your feelings if you are to overcome them. Burying them or blaming them on others are the two ways in which we avoid our feelings.
- Your feelings are only dangerous because you don't trust what the "real you" might do if you let your feelings soar freely.
- Your feelings reside in your Inner Child. When you embrace your Inner Child by *Listening in the Present* to your own feelings, you make it safe for this emotional part of you to emerge.
- We escape our feelings in many ways—by analyzing, blaming, and by addictive, compulsive behaviors that temporarily soothe our inner pain.

Watch for...

- Blaming others for your feelings. This is a tremendously difficult habit to break, and it creates the basis for "punch, counter-punch."
- Blaming yourself for your feelings by beating yourself up in the naïve 20/20 hindsight vision that you *should* have known better.

Try this...

- "I feel x when you do y," right in the moment you are noticing a new feeling. You'll discover that you can express your feelings and handle the reaction that others will give you in response.
- Notice when you first felt your body sensations—they are

your surest cue to how you are feeling and what thought, word, or event triggered your emotions.

- Ask yourself, "What do I need to do for me, in order to feel safe right now?"

When we learn to give ourselves the emotional support that we didn't receive when we were children, we can dare to expose our emotions in the moment. Then we unleash for ourselves the awesome power of our emotions. Our passion to achieve our goals grows and grows. By nurturing our emotional needs from within ourselves, we are not easily defeated. We are strong as we recognize that our setbacks are just what is happening and not a reflection of past failures or of who we are as human beings. Then we are not abandoning ourselves. Instead, we are loving ourselves, which is how we feel good enough to do what's important now for us, no matter what is happening around us.

Epilogue:
Real Life, Real You

THE PAST SERVES US

When we let past wounds dominate our present lives, we are doing so because it serves us. Holding on to these wounds is how we take care of ourselves, doing what is best for us based on our experiences thus far in life. If you can accept this as true, you will begin to create a safe spot within yourself to dare to examine your unconscious habits and preferences. You will discover what's right for you by being aware that *whatever* you are saying, doing, thinking, and feeling reflects what's important now for you. To take notice of what's happening within yourself as you live your daily life, is to live fully in the present. As you do, you will begin to see how your past wounds are interfering with your ability to be fully present in mind, body, heart, and soul.

Nowhere is this more noticeable than when you have

done something of which you feel ashamed. Shame is blame directed at yourself. Even when you want to blame someone else for a past event, (he raped me, she dumped me, they misled me, and so on), deep down most of us also blame ourselves. A voice within says, "Why did I go out at that time of night in that dangerous part of town? Why did I give my heart to someone who would treat me so badly? Why did I trust that lying bastard?" In order to let go of the past, you have to come to peace with these moments that you view as "mistakes."

Let's look at an example of this. We could look at small "mistakes," such as making a wrong turn while driving, to big "mistakes" such as a divorce trial or a meeting with the boss at which we end up getting fired. The principles are always the same, so I will choose a medium-sized "mistake," such as causing a car accident.

You are driving your new van on a busy single-lane road on a snowy, winter morning. You have a nine o'clock appointment. You've left your house at 8:15 to give yourself lots of time for the half-hour drive. You notice that you feel mildly anxious because this is a very important meeting, which could bring big success for you if the head buyer accepts your proposal. You notice a nagging thought, wondering whether this guy really likes you in the first place. You try to calm yourself by running the main selling argument through your mind, trying to reassure yourself that you've got it down pat. Now you are driving down a long hill when suddenly the three cars in front of you come to a quick stop as the first car has stopped to make a left-hand turn in the face of heavy traffic coming in the other direction. You instantly jam on your brakes to avoid hitting the car in front of you, but the road is slippery and you know that you won't make it. You decide to swerve to the right while braking hard. Your car misses the other cars and slides through the intersection to the right of them. Luckily, there is no one coming at you from the right hand road. You immediately see a telephone pole, a fence, and a steel post. Somehow you avoid hitting both poles as you slide over the curb, through the snow bank and, SLAM!—right into the fence. The jarring sounds of the fence post and rails snapping, along with the crunch and tinkle of broken glass and bent steel, fill your ears. You quickly glance in the rear-view mirror to see if anyone is about to ram into you. No one is behind you, and so you jump out of your van, feeling a little in shock. As the situation gets under control, you think, "Damn! I can't believe it!" as another driver runs over to see if you are all right. Then your mind leaps ahead to your upcoming meeting that you now figure is a lost cause.

Let's freeze this moment. What's happened inside yourself during that fifteen-second situation? Your body's adrenaline skyrocketed, your palms became sweaty, you white-knuckled your grip on the wheel, while your chest grew tight. You felt a moment of panic as you felt yourself losing control of your van. Time seemed to slow down as you noticed the cars stopped in front of you, slammed on your brakes, felt the sliding of your tires on the icy pavement, and steered yourself to a stop. You made instant decisions, and you successfully avoided what might have been a much uglier multiple car pile-up.

How you react to this event will show you what you believe is important now for you. What you actually do will be the evidence of what you currently *believe* is right for you. You might react by second-guessing yourself. "How could I have been so stupid to be driving so fast on such an icy day!" "Why did I take our new van today of all days, when usually I drive our beat-up old car?" "This will probably cost me two thousand dollars to repair, plus fixing that guy's fence!" "My boss is going to be upset when I tell him what happened." Your stomach sinks as all the ramifications of this accident begin to sink in. Beating yourself is what's important now for you. Old tapes lodged deep in your memory banks begin to play, reminding you of what a failure you are and how only "bad" people make mistakes such as this one.

How would someone who is living fully in the present react in this situation? Their first reaction would be acceptance. They would have already let go of the losses around the damaged fence and car. That is already in the past. Nothing on earth will undo the damages. Any grieving would happen quickly. Then they would consider the possibility that attending their meeting might still be possible. What's important now might be to get to that meeting, unfettered by what just happened. To feel clear-minded to this degree, they would have let go of the significance of the meeting. By getting to a phone, they might make the necessary calls to get a ride or delay the meeting. Then they could attend to the details of dealing with the police, the fence owner and their own car repair. They would feel comfortable at the prospect of facing their boss, knowing that their driving record is not a reflection of their competency to do their job.

Most of us aren't that perfect. How could some of the doorways to present living be helpful to people who beat themselves up instead? Perhaps they could let go by *being grateful*. "Thank heavens, it's only my van that got damaged, and that no one was hurt." They could *reframe their beliefs*. Instead of believing that "only idiots cause accidents," they might decide that "having an accident does not make me a bad person." Then they will feel ready to face any *disapproving* questioning they might receive, from the hurtful teasing of work colleagues to the frowning look on their wife's face.

They could *let go of outcomes* by deciding that they'll give up the Florida vacation they were planning with their family in order to pay for the van repairs. The vacation was never real in the first place, they remind themselves. Then they might *feel their feelings*. They might connect to their Inner Child and sense out whether he/she feels safe, scared, sad, or mad. A sense of sadness might pour through their body as they grieve the loss of the vacation and the disappointment their family will surely feel. They trust themselves, however, that they will *Listen in the Present* to their family members' hurt or angry feelings resulting from that loss. They know that their feelings *are not about them*, and so they will be able to *mirror* back their feelings with *empathy*, creating a safe environment in which everyone can explore new ways to have a winter holiday in light of this unexpected setback. They might even ask themselves, "I wonder why the universe is giving me this experience today?" as new lessons for learning what's important for them emerge from this unexpected turn of events. Maybe there is a silver lining already showing itself, as they return to feeling calm and centered within themselves, present to what's important for them in light of this accident, and ready to handle whatever consequences and outcomes lay ahead.

These techniques can be applied to any situation that is now in the past. The essence of letting go of the past comes from accepting that the past is often locked into a past fantasy about a future dream that is no longer going to happen. The emotional loss from the car accident may really be about a person's future expectation that they would have a shiny new van for several years to come, and that they would get to go on a Florida vacation.

In that same way, the divorce of the past is perhaps anchored in a dream about raising children, building a home, and having a happy retirement. The death of a loved one is anchored in hopes of shared future dreams of graduations and Christmases that are now gone. The loss of a business contract, a job, or an important sports game are all tied in with dreams of future glory that will no longer happen in the way that you expected. Once you grieve that loss, you open yourself to seeing new ways to make the most of your present opportunities in ways that you perhaps never dreamed possible. Such is the gift and the adventure of living in the present.

TRIGGERS

As mentioned in Chapter Two, **Change Your Beliefs**, triggers occur when you notice yourself suddenly having a feeling about what is happening. If you are very present, you will notice the feeling the moment the situation is happening. If you are disconnected from your feelings, you might not notice how truly upset you were until a while later. Triggers are like warning lights that warn you of impending danger or alert you to delightful joy.

While most people tend to think of emotional triggers as negative (oo-oh that guy made me mad by the way he treated me!), they can also be positive. Watching a "hero comes to the rescue" type-of-movie has the intention by the filmmaker of triggering you to feel good about the hero and his courageous actions. "Wasn't that amazing?" you exclaim to your friends afterwards. "I loved that part where he climbed the side of the prison wall, swung across the prison yard on a tiny rope, and smashed through the window of the guard house to save Penelope." Then one of your friends scornfully says, "Ah-h, that was so fake! There's no way a guy could toss a rope onto that rooftop and make it stick! He would have fallen flat on his face!" Your friend wasn't triggered in the way the director wanted. Instead, he was triggered by his perception that the director had failed to make that scene real enough for him.

If you want to know what you unconsciously think is important now for you, all you have to do is notice what triggers you, either positively or negatively. Each time that you expose yourself to situations that push your buttons, you give yourself the opportunity to uncover beliefs that tell you what you *believe* should be happening rather than what *is* happening. I participated in several classes at The Option Institute that were designed to do just that, with the intention of helping us come to peace about each and every trigger that we felt. One time, we did a class in which we focused on "swear words." Swear words are an excellent source of triggers. When someone says to you, "You cunt!", that triggers most people. We collectively agreed that this word was one of the nastiest in the whole of the English language. Our instructors wanted us to reframe our beliefs to see how it was a word like any other word, and that it only had power because we gave it power. So we took turns saying that word in loving, playful, fun ways, over and over again. Soon, I could feel the knife-like reaction I usually felt at the mention of that word, turn into a neutral feeling. We carried on and did the same with a whole long list of these words. By facing them, rather than avoiding them, I found that I could overcome their power and let go of my own instinctive desire to use those words in some moments of anger, thereby feeling safe and centered even if someone were to throw those words at me in anger.

Another hot button for most of us is money. Few people I know will authentically and easily disclose how much money they make. Many people don't like to disclose how much they spend, either! If you make a lot of money and go around telling people, "I made $200,000 last year," well, other people might take offense. They might get triggered and react by saying or thinking, "Goodie, goodie for you. Do you think that makes you special?" At Option, we were once asked to pin on our chests a sheet of paper in bold figures with how much money we made the previous year and the value of our net assets. What a way to uncover buttons! One guy refused to disclose the information at all. I noticed that I immediately assumed he must have so much money that he wanted to hide that fact. Another forty-five-year-old man had an income of less than $5000, and a net worth of zero. I noticed myself feeling triggered by him as I had thoughts of what a bum he must be. Then, of course, I caught myself ("Bad thought, John!") and tried to imagine instead how he had gotten himself into that pickle. But in truth, I learned that what was important now for me was to judge those people based on their money situation. As for myself, I made $60,000 the previous year, which was the second-highest income in the class. Instead of feeling good about that, I felt ashamed. I had made $250,000 the year before that, and I was aching to explain to everyone what my "real" earning potential was. I discovered that how much money I made defined a big part of my self-worth as a person.

How people listen to you can also be a big trigger. If you are conversing with someone, and they are constantly losing eye contact with you by looking over your shoulder or around the room, you know that what's important now for them is not you! As they mumble in a phony way, "Oh yeah. That's interesting. Uh-huh," how you react will tell you what's important now for you. If you are triggered by their lack of interest, you might feel judgmental about them ("What a lack of manners!"). If you are authentic, you might speak up. "Do you *mind* paying attention to me while I am speaking to you?" I might argue that this phrase with that tone of voice is your attempt to fight. You were triggered, and now what's important for you is to *make* the other person listen to you. Of course, if you are speaking to the company president, you might not have that much courage. Instead, you might say, "I feel thirsty. I think I'll go get a drink. Nice talking with you," and inauthentically slip away, mirroring back to yourself that what was important now for you was to take *flight*. If you are fully present, then you would not feel triggered by his inattention. Instead, you would know that his reaction is not about you. Then you would feel much clearer about what's right for you. You might follow his distraction by saying, "I'm intrigued by what you are trying to see. What's happening over there?" Or, you might simply self-disclose how you feel, "I'm feeling like I've lost your interest. Would you like to have this chat another time?"

When you are truly indifferent to what choices the other person makes, yet interested in what's happening for them, you are in the "present zone." What they are doing is not unconsciously triggering past memories of other times when your parents or close friends appeared to be judging you about how much you talk, how well you tell a story, how much money you make, or what you are wearing. Then you will not feel self-conscious about what you are saying or doing, and you will not feel a desire to judge what others are saying or doing. The path to this wonderful place is through facing and then overcoming your triggers. This will feel like effort at first, just as any new skill or way of doing things does. Even this in itself will indicate a trigger for you, one that I felt myself. I had a belief, "Learning should be fast and easy," that resulted in my feeling irritated and frustrated by the time I was dealing with my fiftieth or one hundredth trigger. Instead, I began to accept that I had potentially thousands of triggers and that I always had a choice of facing them or just burying them. Which one I chose depended on how important it was for me to feel centered and present in a particular kind of situation. With time and practice, however, I found that I became quite skilled at noticing my triggers and digging underneath them to discover what beliefs were blocking me, from dealing with flubbed golf-shots, to finding the courage to make cold-calls on the phone for my consulting business.

My instructor at Option once helped me and other students look in the mirror at our triggers by asking us to think about all the times we had given something to others without expecting anything in return. I love this question because when we are fully present, we do what is right for us for our own reasons, and not to receive an outcome or payback from others. As I pondered the question, I thought of times when I had helped people. I felt a little ashamed as I came up with quite a short list. Mostly, I could see that I was doing things to either return a favor or to win a favor for my future use. I decided to call these "you owe me" points. Collecting "you owe me" points is a powerful way to let the past overshadow the present. "You owe me" points are useful because you can cash them in at crucial times when you need a favor. All you have to do is remind the other person of the "sacrifice" you made for them. I found this especially useful at work if I needed speedy attention to one of my priorities from someone. Collecting these points is a way of carrying the past into the present.

Of course, if you are the one asking for a favor, you are at risk that someone else will now have a stash of points with your name on them. They can come calling at any time, and if their request doesn't suit you at that time, you are faced with a tough dilemma. Do you dare to be authentic and risk their wrath, or do you cave in because you *owe* them? Being in debt over "you owe me" points is one of the main reasons many of us struggle to accept gifts and favors from others. Some of us would much rather give than receive because then we feel free of emotional debts and obligations. No one can use our past against us to make us feel guilty or to manipulate us into doing things against our will. When you have the habit of using consequences to get what you want, you are essentially playing the "you owe me" game. This is a way to feel in *control* of the present moment by being able to "force" others to conform to your idea of what the present moment should look like.

The result of "you owe me" points is an accumulation of triggers. You will begin to resent the other person if whatever you ask for always comes with a future price tag. You may inflame the other person if you are the one using your points to get what you want. The only way to get rid of this potential mountain of triggers is to be true to what's important for you, irrespective of past debts or future credits. If you helped someone, ask yourself what your motive was. If you just wanted to be helpful, you'll know your truth the next time you ask them for help and they say no. In that millisecond, you'll know whether your past favor to them flashes across your mind as a debt they owe you, or whether you can accept that their rejection of your request is not about you.

Ultimately, triggers are means by which you try to *fight* to get what you want, or *flee* to avoid what you don't want. Many of us avoid triggers by escaping from our feelings. We don't want to feel the pain of the sense of rejection, abandonment or attack that each trigger cuts us with deep down. When you can truly feel your feelings, you will notice each and every trigger you feel, even if there are dozens of them everyday. This is what can make this a difficult journey. Once you can feel your feelings clearly and immediately, sooner or later you will want to deal with them rather than ride this kind of wild roller coaster everyday. Your desire to overcome them will be what leads you to discovering what's really important for you in this present moment.

APPLYING "LISTENING IN THE PRESENT"

The most powerful way for discovering the barriers that stand between you and living more fully in the present, is to *Listen in the Present*. This extraordinary technique is a way to check yourself, in the same way that a gauge on a car will tell you how well the battery is charging, or whether the electrical system is working properly. You can do it anytime, anywhere, as long as you have someone else with you who wants to talk with you.

First, you must separate *Listening in the Present* into its four steps, working on each step separately and distinctly in order to master it—**M**irror—**E**mpathize—**A**ssert—**D**o. Then you must apply this approach to situations that are progressively more challenging. I would like to give you three examples to illustrate how *Listening in the Present* is an effective way to stay centered and present, and how it can help you become aware of moments that trigger you into "fight-or-flight." It is this "fight-or-flight" response that renders you incapable of being fully present and fully connected to what's important now for you. Your unconscious mind will automatically cause you to reproduce past habits and behaviors based on the often false illusion that you will feel safer that way. *Listening in the Present* will cause these habits to come to the surface, so that you will see more clearly how you are blocking yourself from being fully present.

Let's start with an easy situation. Let's say a woman named Anne is meeting with her friend Jane. Jane is an incessant, rambling talker. She wants to relate every gory detail of her life, from what she bought at the grocery store to every stop she made on her recent vacation. Jane is a sweet person, but sometimes Anne finds her non-stop chit-chat a bit hard to take. However, Anne hasn't been very authentic with her because she wanted to avoid hurting Jane's feelings. This time, Anne decides to *Listen in the Present* with her.

"Hi Jane! How are you?"

"Hi Anne! Hey, it's great to see you. I just came back from the mall. You wouldn't believe the great sale they are having on shoes. I went in and tried on *ten* pairs of shoes. I could hardly believe the deals they were offering..."

Anne gently interrupts Jane by *mirroring* back to her what she said. "So you just got back from the mall, tried on ten pairs of shoes, and now you're saying they had some great deals on!" Anne has good eye contact with Jane, and she is genuinely connected to Jane's every word and feeling.

Jane carries right on. "Yeah. I couldn't decide between getting a pair of flat walking shoes, which I've been needing *forever*, or a pair of really funky dress shoes, which I've also been dying to get. The place was packed and the service was just *awful*. They really should hire more staff when they have these sale events. The man who did help me was unbelievably rude. He sat me down, got me just two pairs of shoes, and then took off to help three other customers before he got back to me! Can you imagine? I was there ahead of every one of those other customers, too."

Anne notices how emotional Jane is and begins to both *Mirror* and *Empathize* with Jane. "You were the first one there, and he served three other customers before he got to you? (mirror). No wonder you feel upset about how he treated you!" (empathy). Anne's tone of voice reflects the annoyance that Jane feels. Otherwise, she will come across as mocking or judgmental.

Jane, of course, is just bursting to keep on talking, but noticeably loves how Anne is hanging on to her every word. Anne notices that her *Listening in the Present* is initially causing Jane to really get humming on the shoe story. However, within a couple of minutes, Anne feels that Jane is calming down and actually asks Anne whether she herself needs any shoes. After a bit more conversing, Anne decides to *Assert* herself by saying that she wants to return to work and then promptly *Does* so.

In this situation, Anne has let go of her need to voice her own opinion about shoes, or to discuss a topic that currently fascinates her. Instead, she has decided to be fully present with Jane and her need to talk about her shoe store experience. This time, however, Anne felt calm, centered, and relaxed as she set aside her normal desire to *judge* her experience as negative or boring. She *let go of her belief* that "good people ask me what I'm doing if I ask them what they've been doing." She did what was important for her by asserting her desire to return to work, even though Jane had much more to say. Anne did, however, notice a small trigger when Jane seemed to be mildly annoyed at Anne's abrupt departure. "I wonder if I was too harsh? I hope I didn't hurt her feelings. Maybe Jane will be mad at me now, and wonder why I was suddenly so abrupt instead of listening to everything she had to say." Anne is *replaying* the conversation, second-guessing herself. This is a way for Anne to know that part of her still wants the *approval of others*. Anne knows that she must have a *belief* somewhere deep down that is making it hard for her to be true to what's important for her in some situations.

In the following situation, the potential for conflict is much higher. Usually, these situations occur with someone who has power and influence over you, such as a boss, a co-worker, or a family member. In this example, Jerry and

Sara, a married couple, are debating whether to buy a new carpet or not.

Sara is excited. "A new carpet is going to make this room look fantastic! This old one is so ratty and torn. I can hardly stand looking at it anymore."

Jerry is not convinced. "It's not that bad, honey. It's only eight years old."

"Only!" Sara exclaims. "Eight years of dog hair, and children's dirty feet. Who knows what other creatures are living in that bug-infested mess!"

"Sara, this carpet is going to cost $2500! I don't think we have that kind of money to spare for a carpet. What about the spring vacation we wanted to take? What about the car that's now five years old?"

"I do want to take that vacation, and I just hope that our car lasts a couple more years. You know I've wanted this carpet for the last three years. I can't live with the old one for another year!" Sara is getting emotional, and Jerry can feel himself starting to feel guilty, as if he were being a bad husband by not giving in to Sara. Jerry decides to set aside his concerns over money, a new car, and a spring vacation and to start *Listening in the Present* to Sara.

"You've wanted this carpet for three years, haven't you?" he says empathetically. His tone of voice reflects that he is fully in the moment. If he had said, "I *know* you've wanted this carpet for three years," there would have been no empathy even though he would have mirrored Sara's words back to her.

Sara's face softens. "You know I have, sweetheart."

Jerry responds, "I can appreciate why you feel that way. This carpet does have stains on it, even though we've had it steam-cleaned twice. Even the color doesn't really match our wallpaper."

"Oh, honey! I'm so glad you understand. Let's go out this afternoon and buy it, okay?"

Now comes the hard part. Just because you have mirrored back the other person's words and empathized with how they feel does *not* mean that you are obligated to *agree* with them. This is a moment of truth in which you have the opportunity to authentically do what's important for you. Only *you* know what that is for you. In this case, Jerry does not agree that he and Sara have the money for this purchase. He can respond in a variety of ways, each of which would reflect his current beliefs about what's important now for him. He could *fight* by getting aggressive and saying, "Don't give me that 'Oh honey' crap! You always try to sweet-talk me into what you want. Well, this time, you can forget it! I'm still fuming over that new couch-set and those curtains you bought last fall. There is no way I will agree to buying that carpet!" Jerry is bringing up the past, which is a sure-fire way to flare up Sara's walls. She will feel defensive and seek to "counter-punch" by bringing up other past situations in which Jerry didn't agree to what *she* had wanted, or where she gave in to Jerry's desires.

Jerry could also take *flight* by avoiding the whole situation. "Sara, it's getting late, and I have a major report to finish for work. Let's talk about this later, okay?" Alternatively, he could cave in and agree to buying the carpet, even though he's already resentful about the couch-set and the curtains. Jerry's third choice is to *Assert* what he wants. "Listen Sara, I know this is important to you, but I am not convinced this is the right time to do it. We have a lot of bills to pay off, and I'm feeling scared about my job situation. I just don't want any more debt hanging over our heads." Jerry has asserted what he wants, and he has authentically self-disclosed his feelings without *blaming* Sara for how he feels. He can only guess as to how she will respond. But he doesn't try to anticipate her possible reaction to his stand on this issue by *role-play-thinking*. He trusts himself that he will stay true to what's really important for him. In the end, Sara is moved by his genuine worry about his job, and they agree to postpone the discussion about the carpet purchase for two months. Sara will truly feel listened to by her husband if Jerry then *does* what he said he would do—discuss the carpet purchase again in two months, rather than try to permanently avoid the subject.

This topic was potentially much more explosive than the topic in the first example. The payoff for *mirroring* and *empathizing* is that the other person feels heard. Their walls tend to stay down, their ears open up, and there are increased chances that they will hear the other person, though that is not a guarantee!

Knowing that you can trust yourself to stand up for what's important for you is what will give you the courage to *Listen in the Present* fully and openly. Whenever you lose the ability to *Listen in the Present*, you can be sure that someone has triggered one of your beliefs about how they should be responding to you. Perhaps you are attached to an outcome that matters to you so much that you want to take control of the situation and force it to unfold *your* way. By listening in this way, you will uncover your opportunities to go through several doorways, such as being authentic by disclosing your truth, changing your beliefs, letting go of your desired outcome, or feeling your feelings through the expression of your anger, your sadness, or your fear. It is important to do this without blaming the other person for how you feel. It is also important that you avoid bringing up past "baggage."

When you get into a "hot" situation, you will face the true test of how present you can be in order to do what's important for you *under pressure*. The degree to which you experience stress and anxiety will depend on how unsafe you feel in these kinds of situations. For example, surveys have shown that many people are more frightened of speaking in public than they are of dying! Personally, I used to be terrified by the idea of going up to a strange woman in a bar. Making a presentation to an important boss, or telling your spouse how you really feel about your sex life can also be nerve-wracking "hot" situations.

Let's look at a situation in which a married couple find themselves in this kind of a situation. Carl and Sharon are newlyweds. This is the second marriage for both. Each of them went through the pain and heartache of divorce, and both currently have shared-access arrangements with their ex-spouses for their children. Their children—they have two each—are of elementary school age. Carl's fight with his ex-wife is not yet over. He and his ex-wife keep threatening each other with legal action, as she wants more money from him, and he wants more access-time with his children. Sharon loves to spend money, and Carl is getting very worried as the credit card bills and legal bills mount. One day, Sharon walks through the door with several shopping bags from high-priced ladies' fashion stores. Carl sees red even as Sharon begins to speak.

"Hi honey. You would not believe the deals I got on new work clothes!"

"Oh yes, I would," Carl says sarcastically. "Sharon, just how much did you spend today?"

Sharon is immediately annoyed. "Why is money always the very first thing you ask me about? I looked very hard to get good value today, and I need these clothes. Why can't you just back off and let me feel good about what I've done instead of raining on my parade all the time?"

Let's freeze this situation for a moment. In the early stages of their marriage, this couple has already been swamped by the past. His money fears, her past spending habits, and his nagging at her about money are adding up to making *Listening in the Present* nearly impossible. If they could each feel safe within themselves, they could let go of their frets and regrets and focus on what's important now—creating a safe environment in which to talk about their present issues.

Let's say Sharon recognizes that this is a "hot" situation for Carl, and she moves into *Listening in the Present* rather than being defensive. She takes a deep breath, and lets go of her desire to keep her new purchases. She knows that they are not as important to her as a healthy relationship with Carl, and the possibility of "losing" the argument to Carl does not feel threatening to her. After a pause, she says,

"You sound worried about how much money I have spent."

Carl looks relieved. "That's right, Sharon. I don't want to rain on your parade, but I do feel like you don't take our money issues seriously when you run off and blow another wad of dough on clothes that you don't even need!"

Sharon has to take a deep breath here. Carl has just implied that she is irresponsible about money and that she is wasting it on stuff she doesn't even need. However, she knows his feelings are not about her, and so she is able to stay present with him, rather than jump into fight-or-flight mode. She responds by *Mirroring*,

"You're saying that you think I don't take our money issues seriously and that I have blown a wad of dough on clothes that I don't even need."

She resists the temptation to tell him how wrong he is, how she cuts corners to save money all the time, and how her wardrobe is now three years old. Instead, she patiently waits and let's him speak again.

Carl feels calmer, noticing that Sharon has given him a window to really say what is on his mind. "Yeah, that's right. Last month, we spent a thousand dollars more than we brought in. Our Visa bill is now five thousand dollars. I see all this money going out on clothes, backyard furniture, and kids' stuff, and I just feel like we're wasting a ton of money."

Sharon stays centered, focusing now on empathizing with Carl. "I can see how it could look like a waste of money to you. We do buy a lot of stuff, that's for sure. You sound like you feel a bit scared about our money situation."

Carl drinks in her empathy, but feels a little defensive because he didn't actually say the word "scared," even though he clearly feels that way. "I don't think that I'm scared, but I sure as heck don't want the situation to get any worse. And I want to feel like you're with me on this, and that I'm not the only one concerned about our finances."

Again, Sharon might be triggered here, resenting the idea that he thinks he is carrying the financial load alone, when she herself brings home a paycheck from a full-time job. Instead, she keeps *Listening in the Present* by further empathizing. "I can appreciate that you wouldn't want to feel like you are fighting this battle alone."

At this point, their conversation is moving towards step three, *Asserting*. Carl could assert what he wants specifically from Sharon, or Sharon could ask him, or she could make an offer. In this case, she decides to ask him an open-ended question. "What would make you feel like I'm in on this with you and you're not alone?"

Carl thinks about it for a minute, not quite able to put a finger on why this conversation seems so much better than past ones he's had with his wife. "I think I want us to agree on how much debt we're going to pay off every month and how much money you will have to spend for all the extras like clothes and so on. I want us to not spend more than we make in any month. That's what I want," he says with some satisfaction. Whether Sharon agrees or how they work it out from here doesn't really matter for our purposes. What matters is that whatever they agree to do, they *Do*. They respect and love each other enough to know that whatever they agree on is not set in concrete. The past does not define the present. Just because this is what they agreed on does not mean that it must be that way forever more. Either person can speak up authentically and say, "I want a change," knowing that the other person will respect their wish, and will genuinely listen to their new concerns.

Listening in the Present is the most powerful technique that I know of to create emotional safety within a marriage. And nowhere is safety more crucial than in a marriage. When we fall in love and commit ourselves to our life partner in a long-term relationship, we truly commit ourselves to the "safe yet dangerous" paradox that is the essence of living in the present. We feel safe with our partner, and we share all of the intimate details of our past lives and future dreams. What a wonderful feeling it is to know that what you did, what you want, and who you are, is loved and accepted by that special person in your life. This joy of love has kept the institutions of courtship and marriage alive and well through all the centuries.

Of course, the only way you can have that warm, safe feeling is to be open and vulnerable with your partner. The moment you are, that person has also become the most dangerous person in your life. They can reveal your darkest secrets to other people. They can spend you into bankruptcy. They can bring burdens upon you, such as the need to care for them in illness, or to deal with their family of origin. They can leave you for another lover just when you really need them and depend on them. There is seemingly no limit to the amount of pain that your love partner can bring upon you.

Your partner knows exactly which buttons to push in order to trigger a reaction from you. They know just how to criticize your work, step on your feelings, or take a shot at your mother. They are uncannily capable of asking a question in just the right tone of voice that will get under your skin as you detect their tone of skepticism or sarcasm in response to what you are doing. They know just how long they have to be silent with you before you crack, either in anger or by giving in. These are the ways in which they seek to control your behavior so that they will feel safe. Not that you would ever do that to them...! When you give your partner these kinds of minor jabs or major blows, you are letting the past influence what's important now for you. Whether your approach is *right* for you is the lesson that you have to decide for yourself as you become clear and conscious of your natural, instinctive habits and behaviors.

THE PARADOX OF CHANGE

When you instinctively say and do what you want, based on what you authentically think and feel, you open doorways to discovering who you really are. Once you are able to embrace yourself in this way, fully and without reservation, you become capable of making changes to who you are. This is the ultimate payoff for daring to live fully in the present. By embracing all of you, the good, the bad, and the ugly, you become the master of you. You are in charge of what beliefs you hold, what you choose to say and do, how you react to the disapproval of others, and whether you let your attachments and expectations define your present choices. When you pursue living fully in the present, you face the paradox that the only way to change is to accept who you are in the first place!

A friend of mine, who was the president of a small company with about seventy-five employees, discovered the extraordinary impact of this paradox on his employees. When he took over as president, the company was ten years old and very successful. Its employees and managers were very committed to *their* way of doing business. However, the market was becoming increasingly competitive, and my friend foresaw the need to change their shoot-from-the-hip business approach. As a marketing-oriented executive, he wanted to make the company more disciplined and analytical, so that management would rely more on proven marketing methods and consumer research, rather than make major marketing decisions based on gut feelings.

For the first six months, he tried to get people to see that there was another, more effective way to do things and make decisions. His managers would come to him for decisions, and he would send them back, asking them to consider alternative ways to accomplish their goals. They resisted. Not only did they resist, but morale plummeted. It seemed that the harder he tried to explain the merits and benefits of being more disciplined, the more they dug in. He became quite discouraged. Out of frustration, he wanted to fire many of his key people and replace them with more sophisticated managers who understood the fundamentals of sound marketing. While he ended up firing two senior managers, he knew that he couldn't fire everybody.

After almost an entire year, during which he also did personal growth work, he decided that his approach simply wasn't working, so he stopped trying. This was a very gutsy move. The company had just gone public on the stock exchange. Financial analysts were now calling him regularly for performance updates, while the market for his company's trendy products became proliferated with new competitors, as he had predicted. Despite all this, he stopped trying to *force* his preferences onto his employees.

He decided to go with what they wanted most of the time. Instead of trying to explain why they should consider a new way (his way), he became open to understanding why they were doing things their way, even if he disagreed. Naturally, he began to learn a lot more about how his people were thinking. To his amazement, his people responded to his acceptance and openness by wanting to try out some of his ways. Even more astonishing to him was the big lift in employee morale that started to happen. Positive energy returned to their offices. Results started to improve despite the heavy competition.

What did my friend discover? He discovered the *Paradox of Change*:

"People can only change when they feel accepted as they are now."

Stunning. It's like learning to ski and discovering that it's easier if you go faster, not slower. This is a radical concept simply because it is *counter-intuitive*. Many of us have spent much of our lives trying to change other people. Though it rarely works, we tend to do it anyway. We think that if we get unhappy enough, logical enough, critical enough, and persistent enough, others around us will change and then we'll get what we want.

This kind of *pushing* takes enormous energy. We are usually driven by the fear that if we stop trying to change others, they will never change, and we won't get what we want. Deep down, we have a couple of beliefs. We think, *"If*

I don't at least try to change them, then I won't have done the best I can do." We have a belief that "doing our best" means trying to get others to do it our way. We also think, *"If they don't change, I won't get what I want. Then I'll be very unhappy."* We have an attachment to certain outcomes that define who we are and what makes us feel safe. These outcomes drive our desire to enforce certain expectations on others about how things should be done.

Yet, when you try to push people into changing—do they? Perhaps if you have a big-enough "stick," you can push, nudge, manipulate, or otherwise bulldoze others into change, at least temporarily. Perhaps you believe in dangling a carrot instead. That can work, but perhaps at the expense of giving something away that you would really rather not give away. At work, all this will get you is compliance. At home, all this will get you is resentment. You can be sure that the recipients of your "pushing-and-pulling" will find a way to get even with you.

Embracing the *Paradox of Change* is a decision on your part to let go and trust that whatever happens will be just fine. You are making a decision to stop trying to control others. This is a decision which will leave you feeling very vulnerable. Yet, the *Paradox of Change* is the single most powerful thing you can do to promote change in others. When you are accepting of others as they are now, they will feel emotionally safe. When people feel emotionally safe, they become open to the possibility of change. When people feel threatened or insecure because of pressure from you, they retract into their safety zone. They stick with what they know, no matter how harmful it may be for them to do so.

Over my twenty years in business management, I have seen many managers, including myself, lead their people by using anger and fear as their means to motivate. A friend of mine was having difficulty with one of his senior managers. He sat down with him numerous times, trying to explain to that manager how he wanted him to do his job differently. Time after time, the manager continued to do his job the old way. Finally, my friend got fed up. He called in the manager and explained to him that if he didn't change, his job was on the line. Did that manager immediately jump up and exclaim, "I have seen the light! Thank you for making it so clear for me. Now I will do it the way you want me to do it!" No way. He was paralyzed with fear, and remained incapable of making major changes to his lifelong work habits while his boss was holding a gun to his head. My friend never did fire that manager because his technical knowledge was too valuable to the company. How much more success could he have had with this manager if he had just accepted him instead? How could this executive even be truly sure that his way would yield a better result than that of his employee? He could only be sure of one thing: the result would be *different* than he expected. He could not be sure that it would be worse.

Disapproving of others by the use of punitive consequences is the surest way to ensure that other people will not change within themselves. They might comply on the outside, but as soon as the external pressure that you applied is removed, they will bounce back to their original habits and beliefs like a spring coil. If your business or personal relationships are filled with a lot of resentful compliance, you can be sure that sooner or later, one or both of you will want to return to doing your preferred habits in spite of all the pressure to do it differently.

Negative consequences trigger deep fears in us if we have not let go of our attachment to outcomes that we value. The thought of being fired, for example, triggers our fear of being abandoned. We may fear that we will run out of money, which is our basis for survival. Even having our careers derailed by falling out of favor politically triggers our fear of having no friends. This is a major basis of feeling loved. Employees who become "politically" tainted feel like the nerd at school that no one wants to hang around with. This can feel even worse than being fired. Yet if someone fears being abandoned, it is unlikely that you can provide enough security and love to "fix" them. The *Paradox of Change* doesn't mean providing a Rock of Gibraltar kind of love that says "I'll never leave you." Even "till death do us part" implies that one of you will eventually be left alone and abandoned. Rather, the *Paradox of Change* means that you will not be judgmental of their habits, behaviors, and attitudes "in the moment." You will accept them as they are, yet you will be authentic about how you feel in response to their actions and what you think is important from your point of view. Your challenge is to separate *their* behaviors from *your* sense of well-being. The effect is the same as letting oil and water separate when shaken together in a single bottle. Each becomes distinct from the other, even though each is connected to and affected by any movement from the other.

That is the real secret to applying the *Paradox of Change*. We think the behavior of others has something to do with us. In reality, they are just being them. We are just feeling the side effects, painful as those might be. We associate our pain with the person, as the source. Logically, we try to eliminate the pain, or increase our pleasure (i.e., feel more loved) by changing the cause. If that person had been kinder, gentler, and more thoughtful, our lives would be better. This is a great delusion that blocks our ability to be present.

Typically, behind this delusion, we have core beliefs through which we tell ourselves that trying to change other people is justified. One major belief that many of us have is:

"If I did it this way, then you should, too." We are triggered by the belief that if others are not doing it our way, then we

are in danger. The way in which the other person writes the report, fixes the machine, or loads the dishwasher feels threatening to us. The reason is that their actions are reminding us of our own past hurts when we did it that way and experienced some negative consequence for it. We can break this habit only when we become conscious that this is our habit. Then we can ask ourselves whether our danger in this moment is actually real, or if it merely reflects our emotions connected to reliving a past wound.

Another common belief that we use to try to change others rather than accept them is:

"If you really loved me, you would... " This sentence could be completed in at least a hundred ways:

If you loved me...

"...you would remember our anniversary."

"...you would know that I need my sleep tonight, rather than meeting your sexual needs."

"...you would be happy for me that I got a promotion, rather than focusing on the fact that I have to travel more."

"...you would appreciate the job that I am letting you keep, by learning that your way of managing people and getting tasks done is not working, and that my way is the better way."

Being accepting of others means letting go of these kinds of deeply ingrained beliefs. This is painful because we are letting go of powerful ways in which we have effectively influenced others to get what we want. Instead, we are being vulnerable and taking huge risks. At work, the risk is often around delegating. Managers are held accountable for results that they didn't produce themselves. If a subordinate performs poorly, it is the manager's feet that are held to the fire. Yet, trying to change their subordinates in a forceful way just doesn't work in the long run. By fully accepting employees as they are in the present moment, you open the doorways for personal change. If change doesn't occur, that's okay. They wouldn't have changed even if you had pushed them. This doesn't mean that you stop inviting them to try a new way. But if they refuse, you are choosing to accept them. In so doing, you give them and yourself the chance to be the best they could be.

At home, this is even more true. Accepting the habits of our spouse and our children is a very difficult, lifelong challenge. As Marianne Williamson wrote, *"The point of love is to make us grow, not to make us immediately happy."*[7] When we find a way to accept the unpleasant habits of those closest to us, we accept those same qualities in ourselves. When we accept those qualities, we are one step closer to freeing ourselves of our false self and embracing our disowned self. When we embrace our disowned self, we discover our lost self, our true self. Only then are we truly capable of living in the present.

SELF-WORTH ANCHORS

Your triggers will lead you to a clearer understanding of who you are, what you want, and how you believe you will get it. As you do, a picture will begin to emerge about how you perceive your self-worth. Personally, I began to see that I saw myself as unlovable. This stood in stark contrast to my previously dearly-held perception that I was a good-hearted, hard-working, honest person who deserved to be liked, respected, and loved. I discovered that part of me was selfish, mean-spirited, vindictive, and controlling. It was only by trying to be true to what I *thought* was important now for me, that this fuller picture of myself began to emerge so much more clearly. It was only in daring to open doorways

---

[7]Illuminata, A Return to Prayer, Marianne Williamson, 1994, 150

and feel my pain and my shame at some of my past actions and broken relationships that I was able to go there.

As I went through the doorways to living in the present, my real perception of my self-worth began to emerge. When I was smart at work, I felt good about myself. Much of my self-worth was anchored in being "smart" in an intellectual sense. I had always been good in school, and the working world further confirmed to me that it was my smarts that made me "lovable." I suspect that this was the main reason that my collapse on the floor in the family room was such a wake-up call for me. What use would I be to anyone if my brain were so burned out that I couldn't perform my job? I could see my income shriveling up, my wife wanting to leave me, and my friends drifting away. At a deep, unconscious level, my self-worth, my sense of having a purpose and my "loveableness" were inextricably tied in with my intellectual prowess.

As I explored my triggers, I began to see that I was seriously out of balance. Very little of my self-worth was linked to my physical self. I cared about my body only to the extent that it performed its job. However, for a lot of people, this is not true. When you are dating, performing in the public eye, or merely trying to get ahead, how you look can have a profound effect on your sense of self-worth. People with physical deformities, those who are obese, or those who perceive themselves to be a visible minority often have huge triggers around their sense of physical self-worth.

On the other hand, how well I performed athletically was a major trigger for me. I wanted to be an excellent athlete. Eventually, I left most sports behind for golf, which began to consume my time and passion as I strove to become an excellent golfer. Ironically, my inability to be present while playing golf proved to be my biggest barrier to becoming a good golfer. In that respect, golf proved to be a very effective way for me to see how my self-worth was linked to my ability to hit a golf ball well. I needed to break the link between my performance and my sense of self-worth. I needed to eliminate those beliefs that said when I mis-hit the ball in front of a crowd on the first tee, I was not a good-enough person. Only then could I let go of my desired outcome of hitting a perfect shot off the tee, and focus on what's important now in golf—my swing. Where the ball goes afterwards is not in my control.

In the same way, how others react to your physical self is not within your control. If someone is prejudiced about your skin color, the shape of your body, your height, your teeth, or the smoothness of your skin, it's not about you...unless you are triggered by that. Then part of your self-worth is anchored in your physical self and ultimately in feeling unsafe in the face of the disapproval of others.

Some people derive much of their self-worth from their *emotional* prowess. I wasn't one of them. Indeed, I totally distrusted my emotional self. When I made a career change from head of marketing to head of sales, I experienced the shock of my life. Suddenly, my analytical and strategic skills that had anchored my sense of being good enough were of much less value. My ability to win over my customers and build a relationship with them, while still working on getting the order, was everything. My anxiety skyrocketed as I tried to be good enough without being able to rely on the use of my favorite anchor, my intellect. This, of course, made it just that much harder for me to build an emotional connection with my customers. My new job threw me face to face with my tremendous fear of feeling my feelings. Unconsciously, I was afraid that they would see the real me, hiding behind the big title I had in that job. I responded by shutting down (flight) in order to avoid what I instinctively believed was right for me—to blow up with rage at them for not doing things my way, for not seeing the wisdom of my proposals. Ultimately, I was angry with myself for putting myself in that very uncomfortable job (fight).

On the other hand, many people's self-worth is firmly anchored in their emotional prowess. They have the charm, the sensitivity, the good humor, and the warmth to win people over to them. They know that they are liked regardless of whether they are intellectual geniuses or great athletes. Their emotions get them what they want. They know how to make other people feel good, listening to them with great enthusiasm, and giving them sincere compliments. Others feel good about this and are often willing to repay such emotional kindnesses by giving these people what they want.

Your emotional self is a powerful self-worth anchor. The roadblock to living in the present when you rely on this self-worth anchor occurs when something goes wrong and others get upset with you. Since your sense of self-love is linked to whether or not people like you, you will feel in grave danger if they don't. Then you will want to fight or take flight, lashing out at them or abandoning them altogether.

Anchoring your self-worth in your physical talents, your intellectual prowess, or your emotional magnetism, all have shortcomings. While each of them has an important place in our lives as part of the four dimensions that comprise a human being, all of them depend on external feedback to tell us whether what we are saying or doing is good enough. Since someone will always be faster, smarter, and more likable than we are, we will always be comparing the present moment against our expectations and beliefs about how good we *should* have been.

Ultimately, you can only truly know what is truly important for you when you are able to *separate* your sense of self-worth from the events and reactions of what is happening around you. This becomes possible when you are open to exploring your spiritual dimension. It is within your soul that your sense of destiny and purpose lie. When this is clear, what's important now for you will also become clear. This purpose will be bigger than the mere accumulation of wealth, or the approval of others in the form of friends, lovers, and relationships. Indeed, it will be the means by which you will *know* in your soul that you are making a difference in this world. Uncovering this will put your life in perspective and ease you away from wanting to regret the past. Instead, you will have your own internal beacon, acting as a lighthouse that will guide you in deciding what's important for you in the present moment, regardless of what other people expect you to say or do. When this becomes clear for you, you open yourself up to a wellspring of inner strength to be true to who you really are, even in the face of enormous calamities and danger.

This doesn't necessarily mean that you are meant to bring about world peace or solve world hunger. Maybe your purpose is to raise your children to be emotionally centered, productive, adults. Maybe your purpose is to sell a product or service that is making a positive difference in our world. Whatever your purpose is, you will know it when you feel a desire to *serve*, rather than to be served. You will want to give what you are doing without needing a certain response, feedback, or result that feeds your self-worth. After all, you are doing what's important for you, and what happens later is not in your control. Then you will know with deep confidence that whether someone treats you right, pays you well, or honors you is not relevant to who you are. Instead, these are merely signposts and obstacles along your path towards serving your purpose for being on this earth.

Our soul is where our Inner Knowing resides, beyond our ability to think and feel. It stands in contrast to our mind, which we use to construct the thoughts about what we would have liked our past to be, and to dream about what our ideal future would look like. Our mind is both our greatest asset and our greatest liability. It gets in the way of our Inner Knowing as we try to replay the past, rehearse the future, and fantasize about what should be happening. Our ability to know what's important for us at this level is limited by our natural talents and by our acquired skills to assess and evaluate a variety of situations. We cannot always *logically* determine what's truly important for us.

Our soul also stands in contrast to our heart. Our heart is where we feel. This is how we notice our belief system that triggers us to whether what is happening in the present moment is good for us or bad for us. These automatic alarms are merely the past alerting us to the possibility that this moment *might* be like the last similar moment, thereby leading to a scary future. We cannot *know* that this is what will indeed happen this time. Appreciating this will give us the courage to act in spite of our fears in those moments when we know that our fears are stopping us from doing what's important now for us.

Our mind and our heart are the two common ways in which we decide what we should do now, whether consciously or out of unconscious habit. When we open ourselves up to our soul, we give ourselves a whole new way of deciding what is right for us. We no longer compare the present to what we expected or wanted, but rather we ask ourselves,

"What is the universe, or God, trying to tell me by providing me with this experience?"

"What am I supposed to learn from this or do with this if I am to accomplish my purpose for being on this earth?"

When you are asking yourself these questions, you will have opened yourself to your Inner Knowing. Your Inner Knowing will emerge more clearly when you truly feel free to be who you authentically are, able to face the disapproval of others, and willing to let go of people, possessions, and passions that previously impeded your path. When you dare to feel your feelings in order to overcome them, you allow yourself to connect to your Inner Knowing. When you dare to change your beliefs by eliminating your attachment to pre-conceived beliefs about what *should* be happening, you also open yourself to your Inner Knowing. When you feel at peace with your physical self, respecting it as a key messenger in telling you what's important now for you, you will tune in to the significance of the changes in your breathing, your heartbeat, your stomach churning, and your overall sense of feeling relaxed and centered.

Now you will be able to perform to your highest level of personal excellence, knowing that you are doing what's important now for you. You will feel a deepening confidence that you will adapt to new situations, support yourself when things go wrong, and trust yourself that you are good enough in this moment, no matter what victories or defeats you have experienced in the past.

The journey towards living more fully in the present is arduous yet rewarding. By daring to cross these six doorways, you will not suddenly make your life perfect. Indeed, your life may well become more difficult as you dare to do what's important for you in the face of opposition and criticism. However, you will be uncovering the person you really are, and accepting that person, warts and all. Only then will you arrive at the starting line where you know yourself well enough to dare to be the person you have always wanted to be.

Appendix A
Top Symptoms of
Not Being Present

The Four Dimensions of Balance	Top Symptoms of Not Being Present:
Physical	Your voice quivers or vibrates.
	Your breathing becomes shallow.
	Your stomach is churning.
	Your body acts abnormally, e.g., sinus congestion; kinks in neck; cold hands and feet; constipation.
	Your singing voice is off.
	You experience sexual dysfunction.
	Addictive behaviors, e.g., work-aholism; sex-aholism; food-aholism; exercise-aholism: shopping-aholism.

Mental	You can't remember what just happened.
	You are trying to do two things at once, or wishing you could.
	Your head hurts when you try to concentrate.
	Staring—you are looking at something, but are not really seeing it.
	Obsessing about tasks and goals that are not yet achieved.
Emotional	You are irritable and impatient.
	The little things get to you.
	Poor eye contact with others.
	You feel tense and numbed out.
	You sex drive is low.
	You act impulsively in a way that is potentially reckless.
	You use substances to improve how you feel—caffeine, nicotine, alcohol, drugs.
Spiritual	You feel stuck and cannot make an important decision.
	You feel that life is unfair. Nothing seems to go your way.
	You don't feel grateful for what you have, and you notice what you don't yet have.
	God seems distant and abstract.
	You are trying to control things that are not controllable.
	You feel unsure about your purpose in life.

Appendix B
Twenty Ways to Become More Present

The Four Dimensions of Balance	Twenty Ways to Become More Present:
Physical	1. **Get enough sleep.** How does a two-year-old act without enough sleep? He or she is cranky, irritable, and unable to concentrate. Getting enough sleep is my number-one priority.
	2. **Exercise & stretch.** Anything that demands full concentration of your body and muscles. The more intense it is, the quicker you become present. Be careful, because exercise can also be an escape, just like nicotine, alcohol, work, sex, etc.

3. **Eat a balanced diet.** I ask myself, what am I craving? Often it is vegetables, as I find I don't get enough of them. Try to be conscious of what is going into your body each day.

4. **What is your body telling you?** If you feel "off" for any reason, ask yourself if you are avoiding some emotional pain or Inner Knowing that is causing conflict within yourself.

5. **Breathe deeply.** I do a "wolf-howl" with my mouth wide open, and moving my pitch from very high to very low while gradually opening my throat wider. I get instant relief from tension.

Mental

6. **Stop obsessive-compulsive thinking** by going back to first principles: How important is this "crisis?" Will this particular moment make a meaningful difference in what I am trying to accomplish overall?

7. **Use an analytical decision-making method.** Pros and cons. Keep, start, stop. Run your ideas by others. Seek expert input.

8. **Put off decisions until they have to be made.** There is limited upside in thinking too soon, and lots of downside in mental wheel-spinning.

9. **Slow down.** How do you eat an elephant? One bite at a time. Resist the desire to get too many things done in too short a time period.

10. **Make no assumptions.** Discover how often the assumption you would have made, would have turned out to be wrong.

The Four Dimensions of Human Balance	Twenty Ways to Become More Present:
Emotional	11. **How is this emotion serving you?** If you want to stop feeling upset about something permanently, dig into your belief system to discover why you are holding on to it, and then let it go.
	12. **Be playful.** Any cranky two-year-old lets go of anger once something new and exciting is happening.
	13. **Validate your feelings.** Your Inner Child wants to be heard. Are you there for you? Or do you undermine or dismiss how you are feeling?
	14. **Listen in the Present.** It's not about you. Mirror and empathize with how the other person feels, even if you are the subject of their emotions.
	15. **Patch up relationships**—especially with loved ones. You can't be present if every situation that triggers old wounds from your relationship with someone causes your sense of calmness and perspective to be lost.
	16. **Don't use threats.** Only let others know what you intend to do if you are absolutely certain you will do it. Otherwise, persist in asking for what you want until you feel you must make your own choices about what's right for you, in light of their non-cooperation.
	17. **Whisper in response to yelling.** You make it very hard for the other person to maintain their emotional attacks when you are whispering.

Spiritual

18. **Find the silver lining.** Every "disaster" will lead to something positive. I try to trust that God knows better than I do about what is best for me and for those around me. This prevents leaping to conclusions, criticizing others, and generally giving myself a negative experience.

19. **Seek and act on your Inner Knowing.** Don't rely solely on your thinking abilities or your emotional instincts. Both can lead you down reactive and unwise paths.

20. **Meditate.** This helps you let go of racing thoughts of past events for a few minutes, clearing your mind to connect to your Inner Knowing, where you will see more clearly what's important now for you to feel centered and confident.

Appendix C
References and
Resources

This is a partial list of the works that have touched my mind, my heart, my body, and my soul. I have tried to organize them in a way that reflects how they served me in crossing a particular doorway, even if they were helpful in other areas, too. I have placed some references under more than one chapter, reflecting how they have served me.

Chapter 1, Listen to Your Body

FLOW—The Psychology of Optimal Experience, by Mihaly Csikszentmihalyi, 1990, Harper & Row

Your Vitality Quotient, by Dr. Richard Earle & Dr. David Imrie, 1989, Random House of Canada

Toughness Training For Life, by James E. Loehr, 1993 Penguin Books

Chapter 2, Change Your Beliefs

To Love Is To Be Happy With, by Barry Neil Kaufman, 1977, Ballantine Books

Happiness Is A Choice, by Barry Neil Kaufman, 1991, Ballantine Books

Please Understand Me, by David Keirsey and Marilyn Bates, 1978, Prometheus Nemesis Book Co.

Always Change a Losing Game, by David Posen, M.D., 1994, Key Porter Books

www.option.org The Option Institute, Sheffield, Massachusetts,
USA

The Holy Bible, New International Version (NIV), 1973, International
Bible Society

Chapter 3, Be Authentic
Rebuilding—After Your Love Relationship Ends, by Dr. Bruce Fisher,
1981, Impact Publishers

Getting the Love You Want, by Harville Hendrix, 1988, Harper & Row

To Love is To Be Happy With, by Barry Neil Kaufman, 1977, Ballantine
Books

Chapter 4, Risk Disapproval
Healing the Shame that Binds You, John Bradshaw, 1988, Health
Communications Inc.

Forgiveness, by Robin Casarjian, 1992, Bantam Books

Illuminata—A Return to Prayer, by Marianne Williamson, 1994,
Berkley Publishing

Chapter 5, Let Go of Outcomes
Your Money or Your Life, by Joe Dominguez and Vicki Robin, 1992,
Penguin Books

Ghandi, the film starring Ben Kingsley

The Road Less Traveled, by Dr. Scott Peck, 1978, Simon & Schuster

Man's Search for Meaning, by Dr. Victor Frankl, 1946, Simon &
Schuster

Gifts from A Course in Miracles, Edited by Frances Vaughn & Roger
Walsh, 1983, G.P. Putnam Sons

Chapter 6, Feel Your Feelings:
Inner Bonding, by Dr. Margaret Paul, 1990, HarperCollins Publishers

The Flying Boy, by John Lee, 1987, Health Communications Inc.

Healing the Shame that Binds You, by John Bradshaw, 1988, Health
Communications Inc.

Acknowledgements

I would like to thank the many people who have contributed directly to the creation of this work: My sisters Helen Reuter and Linda Butter, and my wife Joanne Savoie for their feedback on my first draft; my dear friend Mary Lou Van Berkel, who patiently read through three drafts and provided me with invaluable feedback each time; Ian Glynwilliams, Cheryl Dawes, and André Robillard for their detailed and time-consuming discussions with me on the second draft; Peter West, Brenda Demeray, Connie Freeman, Patricia Bibb, Peter Bolton, and Susan Fox for reading the third draft and providing me with many insightful comments; Jean Ferguson for her early belief in my abilities and for providing me with helpful structural advice; Simone Gabbay for her superb final edit; and Heidy Lawrance and Kim Monteforte for their excellence in creating the book design.

I also want to express my love and appreciation to the many people who have made an enormous difference in my journey: My parents, Leo and Anne Kuypers, Pam, The Option Institute, Dr. André Stein, the daring men in his group, my Bible study group, my fellow Toastmasters, and my wife Joanne for helping me to discover what's important now for me. I also wish to thank God for the generous gift of my son Jared, whose first five years of life have provided me with a loving and authentic role model on how to live in the present. Finally, I thank God for giving me the strength to persevere for two-and-a-half years on this book, allowing me to ingrain the very lessons that I have been striving to learn.